PORN AND A PASTOR

PORN AND A PASTOR

The Influence of Porn on a Gen X'er

Beau-James Ouellette

Tate Publishing & *Enterprises*

Porn and a Pastor
Copyright © 2009 by Beau James Ouellette. All rights reserved.

No part of this publication may be reproduced, stored in a retrieval system or transmitted in any way by any means, electronic, mechanical, photocopy, recording or otherwise without the prior permission of the author except as provided by USA copyright law.

Scripture quotations marked "NIV" are taken from the *Holy Bible, New International Version* ®, Copyright © 1973, 1978, 1984 by International Bible Society. Used by permission of Zondervan Publishing House. All rights reserved.

Scripture quotations marked "NKJV" are taken from *The New King James Version* / Thomas Nelson Publishers, Nashville: Thomas Nelson Publishers. Copyright © 1982. Used by permission. All rights reserved.

The opinions expressed by the author are not necessarily those of Tate Publishing, LLC.

Published by Tate Publishing & Enterprises, LLC
127 E. Trade Center Terrace | Mustang, Oklahoma 73064 USA
1.888.361.9473 | www.tatepublishing.com

Tate Publishing is committed to excellence in the publishing industry. The company reflects the philosophy established by the founders, based on Psalm 68:11,
"The Lord gave the word and great was the company of those who published it."

Book design copyright © 2009 by Tate Publishing, LLC. All rights reserved.
Cover design by Blake Brasor
Interior design by Nathan Harmony

Published in the United States of America
ISBN: 978-1-61566-015-5
Religion: Christianity: General
10.03.11

TABLE OF CONTENTS

Foreword	7	Why Won't It Go Away?	43
San Fernando and Beyond	13	A Way That Seems Right	61
Influenced	19	The Christian Community	79
Porn: The American Tradition	25	Changing Things	91
Reaching the New World	33	Conclusion	109

☐Stereo ☐Mono ☐Noise Reduction ☐ON ☐OFF

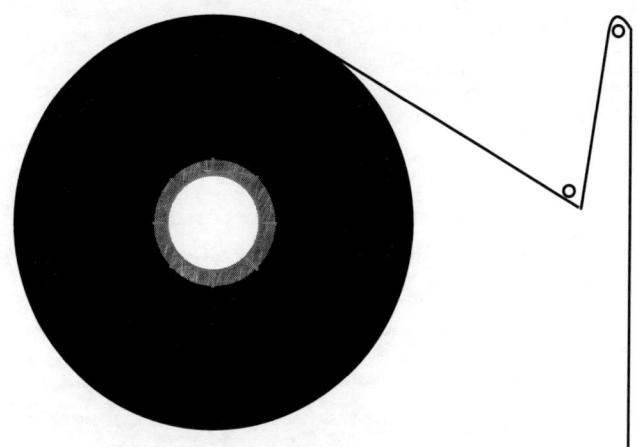

FOREWORD

So why would a pastor want to write about porn? Let's just say that most passions start quite young in the heart of a little lad, and I'm no exception.

Sure, there are many social reasons why a minister could write about porn, and there are those that do. I feel my contribution to the topic is not so much to point out all the "evils" of the porn industry—others do that quite

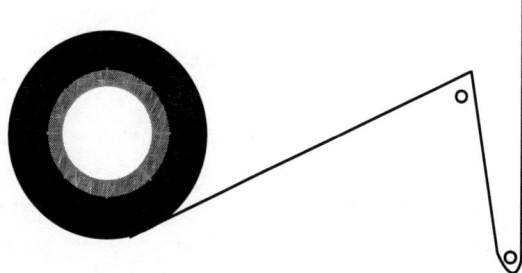

thoroughly—but to give an apologetic look at the topic socially through my own cultural lens.

As I write this, there are current news issues regarding sex on all the major networks: CNN, MSNBC, FOX, and the like. The main actor for *The X Files* has been admitted to a sex recovery house. Christy Brinkley's husband has a porn addiction and had an affair with an eighteen-year-old woman (throws out the myth about porn addicts having ugly wives). Also of note, the infamous porn industry put out a XXX film with the star being a look alike of 2008 vice president nomination for the Republican Party, Governor Sarah Palin, and to top it off, the porn companies want a financial bail out.

> *Girls Gone Wild* CEO Joe Francis and *Hustler* magazine publisher Larry Flynt have said they will petition Congress for financial aid along the lines of what the Big Three automakers are getting.[1]

My purpose for this book is to pass along how porn has impacted not only my life, but the life of our nation and the world.

As so many in our day are concerned about the terrorist without, Al Qaeda, Hezbollah, The Taliban, Iran etc…, when there is one within the home that is doing far more damage worldwide than any cave-dwelling leader could imagine. Could you imagine a terrorist creating a bomb that had the potential to take down every continent at once? An attack that was so thorough that every day, more and more people would be affected. How radical would that be? And so it is. A nuclear bomb can kill many, yet porn kills much, much more.

There are many within the walls of the church that will read this book and think that it is glorifying the life of porn. I would like to respond by saying I have taken much time in prayer and meditation over the written page that might be deemed "offensive" in this small book. I believe that the most offensive and graphic parts to it are in fact Bible passages that I go over in one of the chapters. I have left so much of my own life out of the book. Of course my concern is to honor my parents, and to that end, I wanted my mother to read the rough before I even sent it to the publisher.

My other thought was a question: "Does God use graphic stories (even real life) to expose the gravity of sin?" God is a purposeful God and has included such stories in the Holy Scriptures. I use a few of these types of stories in the book, but the Bible is filled with them. I would never think God glories in the works of the flesh because He has included so much of the works of the flesh in His Word. To use it properly, to expose the gravity of sin in the hope of showing God's power through the grace in Jesus to deliver for the Glory of God, is my desire.

For those that are currently in the battle with porn related bondage, I hope my book will give an understanding that even pastors have wrestled deeply with porn. So many of us think we are the only ones out there who are spending hours at night on the internet knowing we are in bondage. You are not alone. I will show that porn is a much bigger issue than most would want to think about.

But the desire I have is to show that Christ is more

pleasurable then anything that porn can offer. Some no doubt will be taken back by the use of the word pleasure with Jesus, but I do get the idea from the Scriptures (Psalm 36:8 "drink from the river of your pleasures, Psalm 16:11 "At your right hand are pleasures forevermore"). The words that are used to describe a relationship with Jesus in the believer's worship book, the Psalms, use words like delight, joy, satisfaction, taste, drink, desire and pleasure to describe a life in the Lord. I believe we need a change of mind regarding what is desirable and pleasurable, and so I show how porn will never fulfill; for those that watch, and for those that participate in the industry.

I also believe this book is a must for every churchgoer in our country. If not just to open the eyes of a lethargic church, but also to understand that the problem is our own. "Come out from among them" is the call of God's people to the masses that are floating downstream. We are called to be different (1st Peter 2:9) and the difference has to do with holiness and purity. The ball is in our court as believers in Jesus.

To those that do not know the power and freedom that is in Jesus, I hope that you will see a real person who has had real struggles in the pages of this book. Also, I hope you will see the incredible immeasurable hope that Jesus brings to us who are being saved. Will you be a part of such a great salvation? Why would you not want to go against a corrupt world and industry where money is made off of the bondages of other's? Receive the good news that Jesus is better than porn or any other pleasure of this world and embrace the one who laid down his life for you. Serve a master that shed his blood for you, who is exalted by His service to you not by you needing to serve Him! Let Jesus deliver you.

Psalm 50:15 "Call upon me in the day of trouble; I will deliver you, and you shall glorify me."

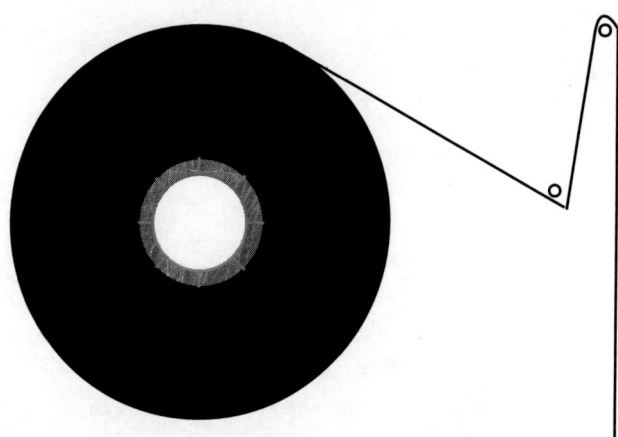

SAN FERNANDO AND BEYOND

Smokeless tobacco is bad for you.... but so is drinking, sex, breathing, pornography, saccharine, and red meat.

—Anonymous

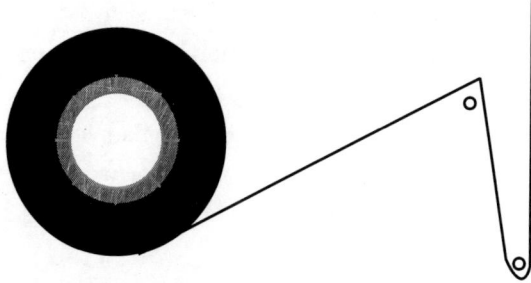

Porn Stars are the New Crossover Artists
Posted by Desi Foxx at 11/3/2008 9:29 p.m.
LA Times
As pornography has evolved from a shadowy racket to a multibillion-dollar global industry based in San Fernando Valley office blocks, top porn stars become just one more celebrity life form among many: dishing behind-the-scenes gossip on talk radio, dashing off autographs for besotted trade-show fans and generally marketing themselves as aggressively as any NBA, MVP, or "American Idol" champ.[2]

I was born in 1972 in Encino, which is located in the San Fernando Valley. My family lived in North Hollywood when I was a little guy with my one-year-older brother. It's amazing that, being so young, I knew nothing of the porn industry, yet even at that young age, I can remember the influence that it had on me in my life.

How many kindergarten kids do you know that look at dirty mags or have seen a porn video? Yet I remember finding *Playboy* mags in a closet at home and remember being fascinated with the pictures. My brother and I went over to a neighbor's house, and I remember our friends putting on a porn video for us to watch. As kids, I remember acting out what I had seen with other kids my age. Even at school I remember smooching with another kindergarten girl in the bushes.

As I became older, I had a conversation with my father about what he did for work when I was in North Hollywood. He said he worked for a book company as a typesetter for adult books. It made all the sense in the world. I always remembered nudity (skinny-dipping) around the house, the parents partying, beer, and some pot. Hey, it was the seventies in the Valley, and the porn industry was getting its thing on. The Pussycat Theater in the Valley was in lights, shocking all those who would dare look up at the titles. Sex was on the mind of the Valley culture, and my family was smack in the middle.

In elementary school, I had girlfriends and was pretty active in the perversion department, remembering what I had seen. It's amazing what we deem normal when we are kids growing up around the influence of porn. Pets are products of their environment, and people are too.

My friends and I were fascinated with porn. One friend even lost his virginity in the same room as me and about ten feet away (I won't say who you are, and I had no clue what was happening). Porn stars John Holmes and Ron Jeremy were like folk heroes to us. And why not? Look at the chicks they're with.

I thought girls that showed there breasts and butts were the bomb. That's what I remembered seeing in the mags and in the videos. I even remember when MTV first came out—wow! All the girls that were in the vids, especially the heavy metal vids, were just like porn chicks but with "some" clothes on. Of course, I gravitated to the heavy metal crowd, if not for the music, for the girls that were around the music scene. Visiting clubs became a favorite pastime for us. I've been able to meet some famous people being around the club scene in LA. We used to go to a club called Bordello where Paulie Shore would attend on occasion. Also, I was on the dance floor with David Lee Roth and brushed up with famous rap star and actor Ice Tee there. On any given night, when you were at a club in the L.A. area during the late eighties and early nineties, there were people that you would know that were in a band or on TV. Of course, girls followed these people, and we were all happy to be a part of the festivities.

As I got older, my girlfriend (later to be my wife) and I became a part of the nineties' rave scene in Southern Cal. If there was any scene that I was a part of that could have mimicked the sixties' love and sex culture, I thought it was the rave scene. I remember my first rave on New Year's Eve of '91 (Xpired was the name). It was in a building in Glendale. I really didn't know what to expect, and nothing I think would have gotten me ready for the next two years. Here were hundreds of teenagers and young people from the L.A. area in a warehouse, on the most touchy, feel-good drugs you could get, and there was absolute harmony in the air. This was nothing like the clubs I was used to in Hollywood. They were small and had a bar and a stage for the bands. This was a giant open room with a place for the DJ and a wall of speakers brought to you by a sound group called the Shredder. I was introduced to ecstasy and nitrous oxide that night, which I would continue to use for the next two years. Now what does this have to do with porn? Think of all the young hormones in these undergrounds. All of us were from different valleys and cities in LA County. I'm sure most of us were influenced by the porn industry growing up. Here we were in one room, dancing for eight hours straight, sweating, and on ecstasy. This was our Woodstock.

When at a rave, it was like stepping into another world. Everybody liked everybody. To see people engaging in sexual behavior of some sort was normal; and I am ashamed to say, we didn't think twice about it. My friends and I got hooked up with a crew called the Savage House Family that promoted raves in the L.A. area and were friends with a musician named Xpando. He was a talented maker of techno music and a great guy. This is really saying something, but in my two years of hitting the underground scene hard, I don't recall ever meeting someone I didn't get along with (must have been the soma). We would help Xpando, when he was going to play a rave, with setting up his equipment and the like. It was cool, and we felt a part of a greater community of ravers. Sex and nudity were so normal to us that during his performances we would escort out a nude stripper, named Flower, who would dance while Xpando played. Quite the duo! I would have the privilege of prepping Flower before the show, painting her naked body. This was not something I thought of as a weird circumstance in the slightest (again, I am ashamed to say). It was a part of the scene. I never thought about her sexually that night or any other. Even when we stayed at her apartment afterward to get rest and she would be walking around the house naked, I never lusted after her. Kind of weird. The rave scene did its very best to promote unity, love, equality, tolerance, and a new age of spirituality with raves named Shiva's Erotic Banquet or Aphrodite's Temple. And for some time, it seemed to work. I mean, how many places can you be where a woman is dancing naked with no bodyguards (unless you count me as one, but that's not a good idea; I'm way too small)? No one approached her nor was anyone shouting vulgar things to her. She simply was a part of the culture in that warehouse. All the youth there had probably seen porn films and sex mags by the time they were in high school. This was nothing more than a painting on the wall to be viewed and admired, but not touched.

All this sexual stimulation and I was just in college.

With all this said, my point is that porn was never something bad to be shunned. Like the quote at the beginning of this chapter, sure it was bad for us, or so we were told, but its influence was all around, exciting and of seemingly great value.

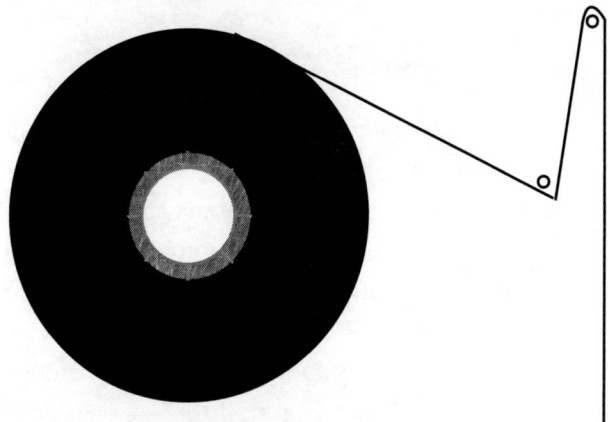

INFLUENCED

I like the quote from Dinesh D'Souza's book, "What's so great about Christianity?" on page 269: "The orgasm has become today's secular sacrament."

I realize that this wasn't the life situation for everyone. Not all kids were raised in the L.A. County area around Hollywood, the sunset strip, Beverly Hills, and Venice Beach, but I would imagine most people in the U.S. have gone into a Wal-Mart or Toys"R"Us or have turned on their

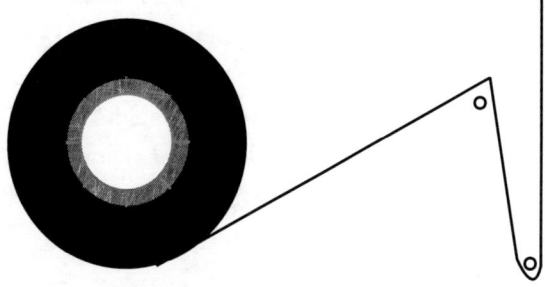

TV or computer. Porn might have had its modern industry roots in the San Fernando Valley and New York, yet today its influence is seen in a countryside house in Maine.

Some people will constantly object to what I am saying about the influence of the porn industry. I probably will be labeled a conservative, Christian, narrow-minded freak. And that's understandable and reasonable. For one, I am a Christian. Right off the bat, your doubts as to my reasonings for writing this book should be questioned. What we've seen are Christian men that talk about porn, but they themselves would never admit to struggling with the temptation or come close to relating the excitement of watching pornography. Second, I am a pastor. This fits too well in this stereotype. But, I am not your normal Christian pastor that has no clue about the life influenced by porn and the excitement that is involved around it. My wife and I believe that we were saved out of this kind of life. We were both involved very heavily with scenes that lead to a secular view of the purpose for sex. It would have taken a few decisions that could have led to some serious different directions for us. We wouldn't have seen the blessing of having our kids or even staying together for sixteen years in an incredible marriage.

I also have objections to comparing the influence of porn today to the past, like in the ancient world of Ephesus where they worshiped the multi-breasted goddess, Diana. The argument is that arousal through visual stimulus has always been around, but I don't think that holds water. Sure, lust has been around throughout the ages, but today we have much more visual stimulation than any other time in history. Just go to Vegas! Or for that matter, turn on your TV. Images are everywhere pointing us to the false pleasure of porn, which I hope to point out within the pages of this book.

A difference today between the our world, and the world of old is that porn is available to all people regardless of economic status. To those that are poor, porn mags are available at a small fee. For those that have a computer with an internet connection, you are open to four hundred million pages of porn, and much of that is free. If you are a teenager with a car, you can attend clubs with go-go dancers, or in college, you can pile in the car with your friends to a local topless bar. But for the very wealthy, it has been the same as in any time in history. Just as David killed Bathsheba's husband because of his lust for her or Solomon needing three hundred wives and seven hundred concubines to fulfill his sexual fantasies, there is always a way for the rich to get what they want and to get a lot of it. Porn is no longer something for those that are blessed with the money needed to have many wives(as in the case of Solomon), but now your average man or woman, teenager or child, can be involved mentally, emotionally, and physically with just as many sexual partners without even leaving the home. That's incredible! What was once only available for kings is now available for everyone.

For those that doubt the influence of the porn industry, I would just ask that they look at the world revenue generated around the world from porn, or they might want to look at the amount of porn pages on the internet. Even in the most unthought-of places, porn is making its impact.

Let's take a look at the latest porn stats in the world.

Currently the industry generates ninety-seven billion dollars worldwide. That's an incredible amount of money. I would imagine that is more the MLB, NHL, NBA, NHL, and NASCAR combined. The U.S.A., to my own shock, is not the leader in generating the most revenue, but China. What makes this most interesting is that China is on the list of countries that has banned the use of porn, yet that has not stopped the country from seeing the potential in exporting porn paraphernalia to the rest of the globe. It's also interesting to note that when finding out what country has searched the most for the word *porn* on the internet, these are the results:

1. South Africa
2. Ireland
3. New Zealand
4. United Kingdom
5. Australia
6. Estonia
7. Norway
8. Canada
9. Croatia

You can also read that in the Islamic world, where we in the West assume there is a chastity belt over those nations, a porn influence exists and is sought out.

All sorts of institutions are in big trouble because

of the internet in Pakistan. People don't really know what Internet and WWW is all about, but they know that they could watch porn images and videos on net very easily and cheaply" By Amna Gilani, Jan. 15, 2008. Category: Entertainment.

By entering the term *sex* into Google Trends, one obtains a ranked list of cities, countries and languages in which the term was entered most frequently. According to Google Trends, the Pakistanis search for "sex" most often, followed by the Egyptians. Iran and Morocco are in fourth and fifth, Indonesia is in seventh and Saudi Arabia in eighth place. The top city for "sex" searches is Cairo. When the terms "boy sex" or "man boy sex" are entered (many Internet filters catch the word "gay"), Pakistan, Iran, Saudi Arabia and Egypt are the first four countries listed.

—"Love, Lust, and Passion"
By Amira El Ahl and Daniel Steinvorth

Pretty interesting.

We all are aware of the porn influence in America and Europe, but just what is going on in these other countries? Also let's look at some of the world's most populated places and see the porn influence there. If the same trend of porn affects their countries as it has America and Europe, then I can safely say that we haven't seen anything yet when it comes to massive porn influence in the world.

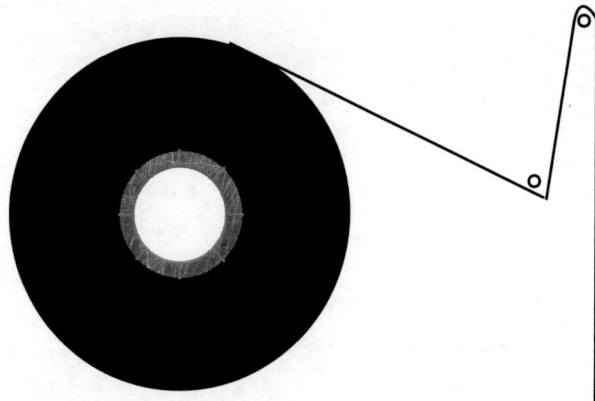

PORN: THE AMERICAN TRADITION

So hard to fathom, the pain in your eyes, as you're watching your people, doing what you despise. In pursuit of our own, we just go round and round. Another nail to our cause, we continue to pound.
—Sean McDonald

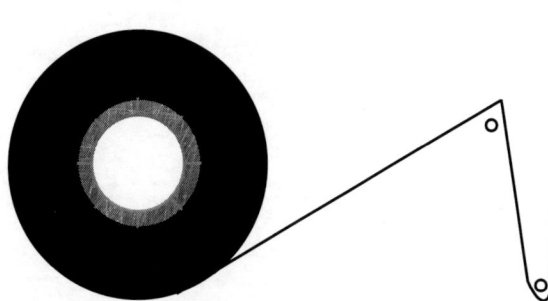

What has the influence of porn been recently in America?

When looking at statistics in the Christian evangelical movement, you can see that it's had an effect. I mean, this is the group that shouldn't be into porn, right? For example, polls at conferences show that around 53% of men at a Promise Keeper conference admitted to viewing pornography *in the last week*.

Promise Keeper men are supposed to be the right-wing, Bible-toting kind of people, right?

Forty percent of pastors say that they have a problem with porn, and fifty percent say that porn is a temptation (I fall into that category).

Certainly in America porn has gotten to us all.

Obviously porn has become much, much more accessible than ever before. We actually don't even have to go far to find it. Back in the old days you had to get up, go out of your house, get in the car, and either go to a strip club or go to a pit of a corner store to buy a mag, and if you got really daring, you might enter one of those businesses that have no windows to rent a vid. Not anymore. Currently the place of erotic worship is right in our houses. Porn takes up 12 percent of the internet at the moment. All it takes is typing in a search word like *lug nuts* and bam!—pictures of nuts. But not necessarily the ones you were looking for.

Out of the 420 million porn pages on the internet, the U.S.A. produces an incredible 244 million of those. The U.S. porn industry cranks out movies at over thirteen thousand per year. That's quite a bit more than Hollywood. I mean, what goes into a porn show anyway? I remember my dad and me visiting his friend's house in the San Bernardino Mountains.

Upon our arrival, we noticed a bunch of cars in the driveway. My dad went in, then came out and said right now we couldn't come in the house; it was being used by the porn industry for a movie. All they need is a house and a day, and bada bing, bada boom, it's a cut. We are the current kings of porn in the world, with Brazil video production coming in second.

It's kind of crazy, but even in the state I live today, we have a city named Chandler in the Phoenix area that made the list of top porn searches on the internet. Have you heard of these cities?

1. Elmhurst, Illinois
2. Meriden, CT
3. Oklahoma City, Oklahoma
4. Irvine, California
5. Kansas City, Kansas
6. Tampa, Florida
7. Chandler, Arizona
8. Norfolk, Virginia
9. Richardson, Texas
10. Las Vegas, Nevada

These are the top ten cities in the U.S. that have searched for the word *XXX* in Google.

So now we know what they're doing in Norfolk, Virginia, Las Vegas, of course, but Meriden, Connecticut?

Everything today seems to be marketed with porn. Just think what someone would say about the U.S. by watching late night TV. First you have the risky stuff, *Girls Gone Wild*, which is a soft-porn infomercial. Then you have male enhancement info galore. I mean, we are fascinated with bigger junk in the trunk. Goggle "male enhancement," and you'll get forty-seven million pages. Man, that's a lot of options. Even on primetime, we have commercials with breasts everywhere. The Edge shave gel commercial is just one example that has chicks blasting shaving cream all over their revealing bodies while wearing practically nothing. This is a great example of how porn has gone mainstream. It's sexual arousal in between your favorite shows. In the book written by Sarracino and Scott called *The Porning of America*, one chapter is called "Would You Like Porn with That Burger?" Porn is now on par with the American hamburger. And this is the point that I try to make regarding my own life. The influence of porn is so heavy in our culture that porn intake is as common as getting a Big Mac.

Just think of the networking sites that have attracted millions of youth. MySpace and Facebook to name a couple. Picture networking sites, blogging networking sites, and the job of keeping them porn free is quite a task. Yet even in the MySpace type of networking sites out there that millions of youth are on every day, banners with girls showing their breasts are endless (not naked, but really close). In my ministry to youth over the past few years, I have seen this trend with the girls' networking pages. They tend to say they're much older than they are and then take pictures of themselves, or have a friend take pictures of them, in skimpy outfits trying to look like sexy models in playboy.

One article I read in Europe was titled "Mommy I want to be a Porn star."

> "I found pre-teen girls who were putting pictures of porn stars on their personal web pages and providing links to porn websites," she says. "I learnt about them through a porn actress who'd published a bestselling autobiography and was surprised when pre-teen girls showed up at signings. They said they saw her as a positive icon."[3]

Yet so many moms here in America dress like porn stars: tight shirts, breasts showing, tight pants, butt showing—you get the picture. I have a little girl, and trying to keep her away from dolls that look like porn stars blows me away. I walk into a toy store, and there they are, little girl dolls with long hair, makeup, big lips with lipstick, skinny, big breasted, high heels, short skirts, and did I mention big breasted? I chuckle inside; it's so amazing to me that I have to detour my little girl from wanting to look like a porn star. Crazy!

But this situation gets even worse. Today you have not only non-porn networking sites, but your choice of porn-networking sites for your viewing pleasure. And it's all for free. Of course, there is always the opportunity to pay for full-length movie downloads, yet most of them, like Porn Tube, which has created quite a stir in the porn industry, are free of charge. Here is an article by Anne Shaw back in December of 2007 titled "Major Porn Company Sues Popular YouTube-like XXX Web Site.

> PornoTube represents a YouTube-like web site offering porn content for all those interested. You don't have to pay anything and your age doesn't represent a problem for accessing the hot videos.
>
> Thus, PornoTube is very popular among XXX fans, who are as well familiar with Vivid Entertainment Group, one of the largest adult film creators of the world. But it seems that the two companies don't get along anymore; unfortunately for porn fans, Vivid filed a lawsuit against PornoTube.

This article shows that the access to porn for free on the internet is seen as a problem even within the porn industry.

And it just gets crazier. Today in America, you can live out your porn fantasy with a real life person for free as well. Adultfriendfinder.com gives you this opportunity by letting you know what they can do for you in bold letters: "Meet real sex partners... in your area, for free!" Now the kicker is this: they boast twenty million members.

So a person in Tucson, Arizona, can sit in his house, watch porn, find a sex partner from down the road, and act out what they saw, all in a night. This is a swingers' club like no other. Porn life and "normal" dating life have merged. It's courting in a whole new way. The average Joe "six pack" can now experience the fantasy for real.

One *LA Times* story carried this title "Porn Stars are the New Crossover Artists," posted by Desi Foxx in the *LA Times*.

Once largely shunned as pariahs by the entertainment industry, porn stars are turning up with increasing regularity on shopping-mall movie screens and in prime-time television shows, underscoring pornography's steady migration over the last three decades from the pop-culture margins to the mainstream.

Even in porn star Ron Jeremy's book, he writes, "Hollywood was a very different place in the new millennium. Back in the '80s and '90s, it was not too common for a porn star to be welcome on prime-time television. But audience's tastes were changing" (page 305, *The Hardest (Working) Man in Showbiz*).

Even in the Christian community, there are ministries set up to outreach to the porn industry. Yet from what I've seen of some of the servants, they look like porn stars themselves. They got the hair, makeup, lipstick, breasts, and tight clothes. I even saw a video on the internet of an outreach in Las Vegas where two Christian ex-porn or ex-prostitutes got dressed up like Vegas' Bailey's girls and went on the strip with a huge sign saying, "Jesus loves you." What a trip! The influence of porn has influenced so much that it has become a ministry tool. Dress up as a Vegas dancer and hit the streets for Jesus.

Another article from Nov. 2008 on the web said this:

> CHICAGO—Groundbreaking research suggests that pregnancy rates are much higher among teens who watch a lot of TV with sexual dialogue and behavior than among those who have tamer

viewing tastes. "Sex and the City," anyone? That was one of the shows used in the research.

The new study is the first to link those viewing habits with teen pregnancy, said lead author Anita Chandra, a Rand Corp. behavioral scientist. Teens who watched the raciest shows were twice as likely to become pregnant over the next three years as those who watched few such programs.[4]

There is no doubt that the porn industry has had an effect in America. How could anyone deny that as the industry generates thirteen billion annually?

By now you are hopefully exasperated by the influence of porn in our country. It is a serious situation, as you can now see. My generation does not see porn as marginal and this influence is only getting much, much worse.

Growing up, I came to view porn as being normal. By the time I was in junior high, I was visiting clubs in Hollywood. Later, in my early college years, I was at underground clubs. The thought of being influenced by pornography was in step with the same demeanor from this quote from famous movie star Johnny Depp: "Maybe I should do something totally different and film a cracking porn with Tim (Burton)." Its influence became interwoven in everything I was a part of and the lens that I viewed life through.

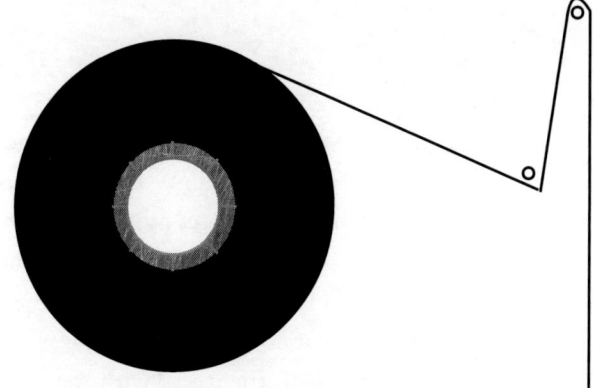

REACHING THE NEW WORLD

Discipleship works, if you work it!
—Anonymous

We all know the impact porn has had on the U.S.A. and European countries, but what about other countries?

Reading Dinesh D'Souza's book, *Why Is Christianity So*

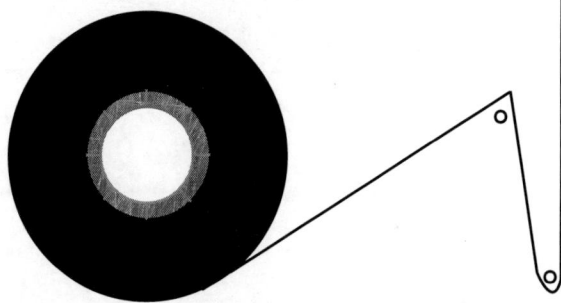

Great? my eyes were opened to the impact that Christianity is making in the vastly populated countries. When the atheist insists that Christianity is dead, he is referring to Europe and the U.S. In these "other" parts of the world, the message of the gospel is growing and reaching people.

Even in the U.S. Christian culture, we are blown away by ministries such as Gospel for Asia, in which founder K.P. Yohanan travels the world with the message to affluent first world country churches: "We don't need your missionaries, but your riches." K.P., with the powerful grace of God, has risen up hundreds of native-born Indian missionaries. The same is happening in China and Africa. D'Souza does a great job giving us a vision of what the impact of Christianity will be like in these countries.

But now think of the porn industry. What if porn were to reach these populated areas with its "good news"? What would the impact be?

In researching a bit, I've found that modern porn in some of these areas is quite new but starting to take off. For the first time, some countries are starting to produce their own porn movies, and governments are trying desperately to filter porn sites from reaching the masses. Good luck!

In Iran alone, the government has to deal with one thousand new porn sites a month. I also read another article from Bangalore, India, about how toon porn is creating a whole new fervor for the young porn viewers.

> BANGALORE, INDIA: There are no dearths of porn sites on the worldwide web. And in India, content with desi flavours are the most sought-

after in the cyber space with lots of sites sprouting up with each passing day.⁵

Pakistan is keen to shield its citizens from the copious amount of explicit material on the web. It could face an uphill struggle, with more than 60% of the country's internet users visiting porn sites, according to telecoms officials.⁶

China has an interesting porn situation. They are on the list of countries that ban porn, yet they generate the most revenue from adult materials exported, such as adult "toys." In an article from Asian Things on the web, I was blown away to read about the growth of this adult industry in China.

> It's a revolution that began with baby steps. In the latter half of the nineties, shops selling sexual aids began opening up in China's larger cities. Unlike sex shops in the west, these places were almost clinical in appearance, more often than not run by frumpy older women dressed in white lab coats. But they did a booming business, and by the early part of the current decade, shops like these had spread from city to city, and even in the smaller towns, stores selling marital aids were popping up. Items that were once taboo had become big business in the middle kingdom, both for domestic use and export. So perhaps it's not all that surprising that Shanghai—a Chinese city long associated with titillation—would be chosen to host China's first sex toy expo.

And if you think people in China aren't excited to see the influence of porn in their country, check out this quote from a famous porn star from California.

> When I got here, I was greeted with a bouquet of flowers by a group of adoring fans who told me that they'd seen a bunch of my movies. All off pirate discs, I'm sure, since there are no legitimate channels to distribute work like mine (pornographic movies are still illegal in China). Still, it's flattering to know that my films are being enjoyed here.[7]

This does not include what is happening in South Africa, which won first place as the top country in 2006 that entered *porn* into search engines on the internet. Here is a disturbing article back in August of 2008 written by Helen Bamford titled, "Kids Profit from Porn."

> Children are downloading hardcore pornographic images for R50 and then making a profit by sharing them with their classmates via Bluetooth - charging R5 each." This is according to Joan Campbell, a child and family therapist specializing in sexual behavior, who said cell phone sex, pornography, and sexually inappropriate behavior among children had soared in the past year. "I have been inundated with calls from primary schools - some very upmarket ones - saying kids are groping each other and what should they do." Campbell, who has been practicing for more than a decade, said that "groping and rubbing up against each other" was prevalent in

poorer communities, but that middle and upper class schools were now calling for help, too. In recent months a number of disturbing incidents have made headlines. One was that children as young as seven were playing "games" called "hit me, hit me" and "rape me, rape me", where they pretended to assault each other. http://www.int.iol.co.za/index.php?click_id=13&set_id=1&art_id=vn20080816083221147C411936

What I find so remarkable about this article is how easily influenced the children of these South African schools are and how modern technology has made porn viewing easy to get for them. But the following comment in the article even grieves me more.

"Campbell said boys often filmed their sexual acts to show them as a trophy."[8]

For those that have been around porn this is the all too familiar way of looking at intimacy, though one of the industry moguls admits to its false pleasure.

In imitating porn, Al Goldstein said people are imitating, "the worst possible kind of sex."[9]

Unfortunately, I think the Euro/U.S. influence in South Africa is taking its toll.

Even the countries in Africa that have a ban on porn, such as Egypt and Kenya, have to deal constantly with the pirate selling and other stealth operations bringing porn to the people.

Now if there is a country that is trying to do away with the daily porn influence through the internet waves, I have to tip my hat off to Iran. In an article back in 2003 from "theregistner.co.uk" by an anonymous writer, the mullah's of Iran have attempted to curve the overwhelming amounts of porn sites by stamping them out one by one, yet are unable to do so due to underestimating the enemy they are fighting. When you think of how many porn sites there are out there in the world, it's astounding! Fighting 420 million porn pages out there is quite a battle. From this article back in 2003, only 8 percent of the population of Iran was surfing the website, "but it is concentrated among the students and those under thirty, who make up about 80 percent of the Iranian population as a whole." Did you get that? Students and those under thirty make up about 80 percent of the population, and most of them are on the web. So maybe I'm safe to assume that in another thirty years, Iran will be entrenched in the internet and porn as well. I think long gone will be the titles that read "Porn actress stoned to death in Iran prison." Really, that did happen. Check out this article from 2001 and the statistic on Iranians searching for the word *sex* on search engines.

"Tehran - An Iranian woman convicted of acting in pornographic films has been stoned to death in the prison where she has been held for the last eight years, a newspaper reported on Monday.

The unnamed 35-year-old was buried in a pit and pelted with stones until she died in the centre of Tehran's Evin prison, the Entekhab paper said, adding that she had been tracked down after an intensive police search."[10]

Iran comes in ninth place in the world.

In Russia, the porn situation has caused a crackdown

on pay-per-view adult programming by the government as read in the following article.

> Domestic media reports say that other providers of pay-TV services are likely to follow suit, and soon enough no TV channels that could be called "pornographic" will be available in Russia, except for perhaps between 1 a.m. and 7 a.m., while those channels advertised as "erotic" will be as innocuous as children's cartoons... Although this explanation sounds plausible, very few people must know whether it's true. But regardless of that, one thing is clear: there is some sort of "crusade" against "pornography" in the media on a governmental level, and pay-TV operators prefer to play it safe while no steps are yet taken—or, probably, they are indeed responding to some kind of "soft warning."[11]

Now let's turn our attention to the country of God, Israel. I mean, if there's a place on earth where the fear of God would prevent porn to run wild, it should be the Holy Land. For any reader of the Bible, you know better than to believe that. Israeli history is loaded with issues with women. King David had a problem with lust; Solomon was a porn addict of the first degree; the nation loved the Moabite women; the prophet Ezekiel told the people to get rid of all their vile images. So here we go again? Earlier in the year of 2008 in an article by Ben Simons titled "Sexy Israeli Festival," Ben writes about the first adult entertainment festival being held in Tel Aviv.

> According to Israeli website Ynetnews, Sextival will be

a three-day event taking place in February organized by former pageant model Nitzan Kirshenboim.

Kirshenboim, thirty-two and a mother of two, is said to have been inspired to stage the event after visiting a sex festival in Berlin.

"I'm actually a real nerd," Kirshenboim said. "I'm just the neighbor's daughter who decided to take the initiative and say, 'Guys, we all have sex; we all enjoy it. Why not get it out in the open?'"

According to reports, Playboy tycoon Hugh Heffner has agreed to allow lucky winners of a raffle to visit his famous mansion as part of a raffle draw.

The event is set to be promoted among some of Israel's more racy media including the local Playboy channel and a local adult entertainment chain store, and Kirschenboim is hoping that both local as well as international visitors will attend the event.

"The Sextival will showcase the wildest things your imagination can come up with," Kirshenboim added while also claiming all interests will be catered for. "You know, some people have a fetish for women with really, really big noses, and this will also be represented in the event. Even those into bondage will find very interesting stuff there.[12]

Sounds quite painful to me.

But did you catch the justification for this event by Kirshenboim: "We all have sex." There you go. That's enough reason for me. I have sex, so why don't we have a festival that shows sex? It makes perfect sense, right? This reasoning alone is quite scary if followed. We'd have murder festivals, drug festivals (oh, sorry, we do—they're called Grateful Dead concerts), abortion festivals…you get my thought here.

Interesting as well is an article about the influence of porn in Palestine.

> Cell phones are selling at a blistering rate. Ramallah is packed with cell phone shops, offering not only the newest Nokia models but accessories like leather holsters and shiny, new touch pads. And the Palestinian Telecommunications Co., the primary cell provider in the West Bank and Gaza, has grown to become the largest stock traded on the Palestinian Securities Exchange, according to the PSE Web site.[13]

Why are cell phones flying off the shelves of shops in Palestine?

> In a place where tradition prohibits premarital sex, young, frustrated men are increasingly turning to outlets like cell phone pornography.[14]

So, like a phrase from the movie *Jurassic Park*, "Porn (not evolution) has found a way."

So I return to D'Souza's idea of what happens when the world's most populated people are reached. Of course, he was talking about Christianity, and I am referring to porn.

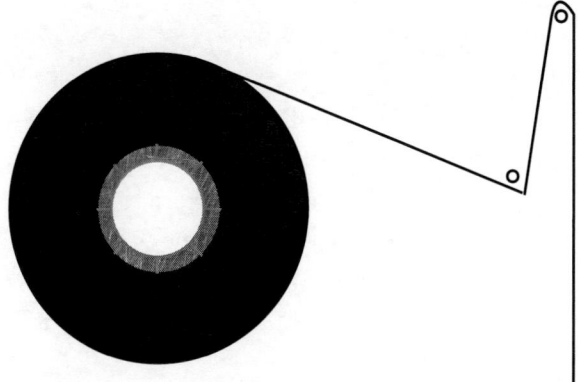

WHY WON'T IT GO AWAY?

C.S. Lewis in *Mere Christianity* wrote, "A man with an obsession is a man who has very little sales-resistance."

"The love of money is a root of all kinds of evil" (I Timothy 6:10).

Cash is king. That's what I hear in these financially interesting times. This might be a bit too simple of an

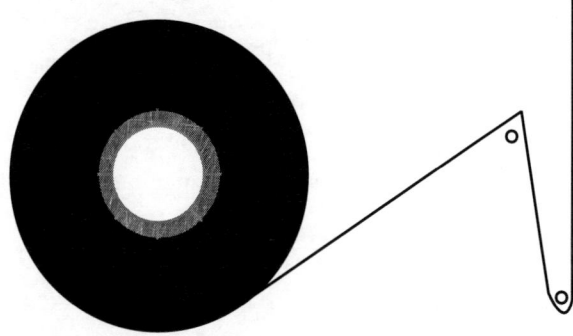

answer, but it really seems to me to come down to money. What would happen in the U.S. if porn production were banned? Could the U.S. afford to say no to thirteen billion dollars? It would be the same as saying good-bye to ABC, NBC, and CBS.

Money, money, and more money is my generation's theme.

Here is something to think about. Look at the industry's leaders and the size of their companies.

> Playboy Enterprises, whose company boasts 2,800 hours of programming reaching a good portion of the globe, employs 725 people as of 2006. Penthouse Media Group has 2 million subscriptions in 45 countries and employs 135 people. Now you can look at the other groups such as New Frontier Media, Private Media Group, Vivid Entertainment, Larry Flynt Productions and Beate Uhse in Germany, which has 1,500 employees, and see that porn is big business. So big in fact that it has its own voice in today's economic climate.[15]

You can also see that if the industry no longer is a player economically, then a lot of jobs go away along with billions of dollars in revenue from taxes for the government. And that's not good news. We in the U.S. have barely any financial backbone, as noted in the 2008 stock market's crash and the panic from the top down.

I found this note on an internet site that ditto's my point.

Porn is one of the few profitable Internet industries, while employing thousands of citizens (The Market and the Industry 1986). Vivid Entertainment Group is one of the world's largest adult film producers in the world, Anti-porn laws threaten to disrupt businesses nationwide and need to consider the legal and financial risks, experts assert. With the size of the industry at $57.0 billion world-wide (now 97) and $12.0 billion U.S., (now over 13) the economy cannot afford the industry being prohibited nor should the thousands of citizens becoming unemployed (Forgione 2005). "It [the industry] employs in excess of 12,000 people in California. And in California alone, we pay over $36 million in taxes every year. So it's a very sizeable industry," says Bill Lyon, a former lobbyist defending the industry" (Porn in the U.S.A. 2004)[16]

In a book written by Pamela Paul titled *Pornified*, she addresses the situation in the U.S. porn industry's lobbyist groups that aim at assimilating themselves into the business world as "just another all-American enterprise trying to make an honest dollar."

This heading is taken from Australia's lobbyist group that can be found on the internet at *http://www.eros.org.au/*:

> Your sexual rights and adult industry are under threat!
> Do you run an adult business?
> Do you care about protecting your rights as an adult?
> Join the EROS Association and help us fight

for your adult business and bedroom rights. Plus get a copy of the EROS magazine and twice-weekly eNews![17]

By the way, the government of the Australian Capital Territory legalized trade in adult videos in 1995. It's big money, and with China bringing in twenty billion a year, all nations have some catching up to do to stay competitive.[18]

There was a really interesting article on the internet on how Americans spent their 2008 tax relief checks from George W. Bush. Whether you thought it was right to get the tax relief check or not, we all were thinking of how we were going to spend it. Most families probably had the Target or Wal-Mart ads opened up and were ready to shop. But wait just a minute. In an article by Corey Lorinsky titled "Where the Government Tax Rebate Checks Really Went: Porn" from July 2, 2008, we read this:

> So far, it seems as though the tax rebate checks aren't so much stimulating the economy as they are Wal-Mart, Exxon, and your food bill. (And soon, Apple, whose 3G iPhone comes out next Friday.)
>
> If there is anything left after that, people might actually be paying down debt and/or saving their checks. And, of course, there's one more way the tax rebates are adding stimulus: porn. From an Adult Internet Market Research Company press release:
>
> An independent market-research firm, AIMRCo (Adult Internet Market Research Company), has discovered that many websites focused on adult or erotic material have experienced an upswing in sales in the recent weeks since checks

have appeared in millions of Americans' mailboxes across the country.

According to Kirk Mishkin, Head Research Consultant for AIMRCo, "Many of the sites we surveyed have reported 20–30% growth in membership rates since mid-May when the checks were first sent out, and typically the summer is a slow period for this market."

Jillian Fox, spokeswoman for LSGmodels.com, one of the sites reporting figures to AIMRCo, added, "In a June 15, 2008 survey to our members, thirty two percent of respondents referenced the recent stimulus package as part of their decision to either become a new member, or renew an existing membership."[19]

How about that? We got the economy going through investing in porn. Obviously, that's a bit overstated and simplified. But I can safely say that the desire for more money is a reason why porn will not go away. Increasing wealth happens in the country and similarly in the porn industry because of us (the citizens) choosing it. Let me try and put it plainly. If I didn't choose to watch porn, then they wouldn't get my cash. If the industry couldn't benefit from my wallet, then they couldn't pay their bills. Our choice to not purchase porn would be the end of the industry. We must admit that everyone receives a benefit from the porn industry as it is a strong contributor to the gross national product, which helps in job production, and in turn money being spent on houses, cars, clothes, etc. Many desire the comfort of wealth no matter what the cost. Many feel bad if someone (even a porn star) loses a job or can't pay their bills, and we believe it's every citizen's right to get a job and raise a family. The industry's success is because of us wanting it. Never mind right now that it is addicting. I'll touch on that later.

Our desire for porn has birthed a 700 ft. giant in the economy called the porn industry. This monster seems to be no longer caged, but on the loose and doing what it wants. We have gotten quite comfortable with this creature. Instead of looking at it as wrecking havoc on the culture, it is seen as a nice, friendly dog, which given the proper attention has amazing benefits. It has become our friend.

WOMEN

I'm switching gears here and want to say something about the feminist movement in the U.S. I can believe that it is the desires of feminists in America to want change in how women are viewed in the porn industry. I mean, for those who don't know, women are bent in every possible way imaginable, and intercourse is had in any place or area with the promotion that it is pleasurable and desirable for the women involved.

But the way I see it is that the feminists have created this monster without realizing it. Before the time of the Enlightenment, where women were seen as property and not on social equal footing with men, women had kids and took care of them. That was the job of women. Just writing that seems so barbaric to me, due to my cultural influence which goes against any critique of women. Now I do not agree with the notion that a woman is property, but I do think there is something to the idea of bearing children and raising them. I mean, it's only been a part of human history for how long now?

In a book written by Laurence O Toole called *Pornocopia*, he adds,

> Porn in the form of regulated materials designed for sexual arousal, emerged partly as a consequence of the decline of religion, and partly through the separation of sex from pro-creation, coupled with views from the Enlightenment that sex might actually make a person happy. Locked in with these ideological shifts were the new theories of gender difference in the West, figuring women as fairer, gentler, more innocent creatures ideally secluded domesticity (page 3).

When we no longer look to women as being special because of their natural ability to bear children, then we look to other indications of her worth in society. I was raised in southern California. Women, to me, were not to be valued for their ability to bear children at all. My culture did not teach me that, nor did my school, and I didn't go to church. The Bible, however, lays heavy stress on this point. Marriage itself was instituted for the work of bringing forth godly children. Malachi 2:15 says, "And why did he not make them one... He seeks godly offspring." In 1 Timothy, Paul the apostle stresses the importance of women in the world by saying, "They shall be saved (not eternally, but relationally) in childbirth." We see women that are pregnant in absolute joy like Samuel's mom, Hannah, and the similar song of joy sung by none other then Mary, the mother of Jesus of Nazareth. This was a normal thought throughout most of history. Women are special and beautiful, not because of the outward (big breasts, full lips, tight body, etc.), but because of their makeup in the ability to bear children. Now, this isn't the only reason the Bible says a woman is special. A look into Proverbs 31 will suffice as my reference, but I want to stress this biblical notion of the importance of women in bearing children, which is seen throughout history, whether in Judeo-Christian culture or any other. This has always been the stress of importance of a woman and rightfully so.

When the feminist movement diminishes this exaltation of women in the way to bear and bring up children in any way, it strips a woman of there numero uno role in the world and puts it on another. For women to be seen as "house wives," there is a thought of "boring" and "not for me!" I have worked with youth for fifteen years in the church environment. . Youth in the church are longing to get out and break free of the traditional ideas that are found in the Bible. Titus 2:4–5 says, "That they admonish the young women to love their husbands, to love their children, to be discreet, chaste, homemakers, good, obedient to their own husbands." There may be numerous books on the reasons why this has happened in our culture, but we all can admit that it has happened. So my first point is that women in today's "enlightenment" culture see their importance in a different way than from the women of old. Instead of their value coming from what they contribute by their ability to bear and raise children, they are looking at what makes them valuable in similar ways as men.

This brings me to another thought, a conclusion from my first point. Just as men have throughout history been seen as sexual pigs, longing for more and more sexual experience, so women have now crossed into the same realm.

Men have always placed an extreme amount of value on their sex life. It is right along with placing our worth in being stronger, smarter, and better looking than those around. We are producers at heart, wanting to show our might through being able to do more than our peers. As a young boy, me and my guy friends would get together and beat each other up to see who was the toughest. Others would have as many girlfriends as they could to show their worth, and still others would try to outdo one another by drinking more. I believe men have always been like that. Not that it is good, because it is not, but we have placed our value in the wrong place. Instead of man's value on his ability to use his strength in honorable ways, like protecting his wife and family, he has exchanged this worth with placing more value on pursuing pleasure through things like sex. Sex is used or seen today predominately in making men and women happy. You might be thinking, "How does that differ from any other time in history?" I will try and use my own life as a illustration.

When I was in high school, it was very normal for a girl to come up to me or a friend and say she wanted to have sex. . That wasn't a shocking statement. In my world back then, it was common for a girl to be as bold as a guy when it came to pleasure and the pursuit of it. Now when I watch *The Blob* or some other old movie, I realize that there was a time where this was not normal. Of course sex was happening, yet the sexual pigs and the dominant attitude for more and more sex was not the normal behavior, but marginal. Girls today do not see their exaltation and worth in what they possess biologically but through the lens of pleasure. *Can I get that guy or girl? Do I look good?* These questions carry the idea of the pursuing acceptance from someone they find pleasurable. There is such an extreme pressure today on women to look a certain way. Most of us sit and watch shows on cable that are focused on how women look, dress and act. How many shows stress the worth of a woman in childbearing and raising children? It's just not valued as it once was. As the quote from Laurence O'Toole said, there is a separation from the purpose of sex for pro-creation. With the advent of birth control technology, lack of religion, and the philosophy of the Enlightenment, the value of sex for a woman is taken from child bearing and replaced in the production of pleasure only. What was once an extreme positive is now seen as a negative in the developed world. The placement of their value has changed.

The feminist have won in this way. They have gotten what they wanted. A woman is no longer exalted for staying with her husband through thick and thin, better or worse, richer or poorer, raising her family for forty years and being a great grandma, but she has become just like one of them, like a man. She can have all the sex she wants with no babies to deal with. Technology has helped this out, no doubt. She can pursue sex as the kings have of old, for pleasure alone. So what should we expect from a girl today who is living in the exaltation of pleasure as their worth? Porn. The feminist movement should not criticize the porn industry and how women are looked at, but instead they should hail the porn industry as their great reward and trophy for a job well done. Women today across the board are valued for their ability to pursue sexual pleasure.

So why won't it go away? Because it would take an army of a movement of women to rise up in opposition to the current climate. And it would also take the culture and the feminist movement to admit that they blew it. Not in all ways, but in this way: by diminishing the value of a woman, by not exalting what makes her valuable (biologically).

The implications on a change of value would result in the end to the abortion issue and, of course, the porn issue.

After reading this chapter, you might be thinking about why the pursuit of pleasure is wrong for men and women as seen in today's culture. In a later chapter, I will discuss why this pursuit of pleasure is not good. To suffice for now, I will end with a thought from a very young instructor of philosophy and pastor from Scotland, Henry Scougal. He wrote, "The worth and excellency of a soul is to be measured by the object of its love."

EVOLUTION

> "We objected to the morality because it interfered with our sexual freedom."

> —Aldus Huxley, "Confessions of a Professed Atheist," *Report*, June 1996

How does evolution affect porn? This might seem a bit interesting for those that are not in the environment that I am in. What does porn have to do with evolution?

Well, as porn star Ron Jeremy says in his book, "I am a bonobo"—a monkey, that is (page 329 of *The Hardest (Working) Man in Showbiz*). And if you ever have seen the TV shows about the bonobo (a.k.a. sex monkey), you know what I mean.

Yet there is a teaching that has preceded the current porn influence in the world, and it is the influence of *evolutionary* thinking. This, I believe, is a cause for the influence of porn worldwide. Before you close the book and say, "Ah, forget this. It's just a creationist," please hear me out on this.

My generation was titled "Generation X." I'm not sure what that meant, but growing up I thought that it meant we liked X-rated movies. Searching the internet, you'd find something like this:

> While the baby boomers had a placid childhood in the 1950s, which helped inspire them to start their revolution, today's gen Xers grew up in a time of drugs, divorce and economic strain…They feel influenced and changed by the social problems they see as their inheritance: racial strife, homelessness, AIDS, fractured families and federal deficits.[20]

One thing that is not mentioned in this or any other discussion about my Generation X brothers and sisters is that we were educated totally by evolutionary thought. I did not hear the words *creation* or *intelligent design* until I was in my twenties. And when I stepped into college, God forbid if someone in the class actually believed in a creator. How foolish and stupid that kind of talk sounded in the classroom. Today, there is much skepticism concerning neo-Darwinism (i.e. the documentary *Expelled*), but in my classroom days, there was an absence of intellectual opposition to it. So there we were, happy to be alive in this world of evolution.

Put yourself in our situations. We were told we came from monkeys and that how we got that way was by our ancestors dominating their species by "survival of the fittest" and "spreading our seed around." That sounded pretty cool as a teen. I was in a crew that could fight, so we had the survival of the fittest thing down, and the next on the list was to spread the seed around, and to our hormones that meant sex, sex, and more sex. Of course, we didn't want the responsibility of a baby, so having sex and finding out how not to have a baby was the way to go. The porn industry seemed to have great success at it. These people had sex for a living and didn't get pregnant (or so we thought), so it could be done.

With our monkey mentality, I thought, *Who would ever want to get married? How lame is that? What's the point? And if you are to get married, why just to one person? That certainly isn't spreading the seed around and dominating the species.*

Now that's from my personal experience. Some of you might have been around strong moral families that helped negate some of the teachings of evolution received in school. But regardless of your moral fiber, we all have been taught (if my age and younger) that evolution is a fact. You and I have descended from the hairy "people" we see in the jungles of Africa on the Discovery Channel.

Saying it is not would be, as Huxley said, "interfering with our sexual freedom." So the teaching of evolution has an effect in which we think porn is okay. I believe so much of today's views of sex hinge on this evolutionary worldview that has played a role in the growth of porn.

It is entirely impossible to tell a teen or an adult that porn is wrong if they believe in evolution. It would make no sense to them. It didn't to me! How could porn be wrong? All I am doing is watching people pursue pleasure. Sure, I'm not spreading my seed productively, but who's to say I won't start?

And so the parents who live God-fearing lives with morality first and foremost feel like beating their heads against the wall when trying to communicate to their youth that porn is not good. First, they would have to engage the youth with what is being taught in school—namely evolution—and debunk it before moving on to the idea of being moral.

Our youth are savvier today. They know the arguments. All kids have been raised on Judge Judy, Dr. Phil, and Law and Order. They argue quite well. It seems utterly ridiculous to argue the destructive nature of porn on a culture when on the other hand they have no basis for a solid morality. Again, porn-looking sex works for the bonobo. Right?

When we place our value of sex on today's scientific world may I say we have no room to argue against porn at all. The scientific world is an ever-changing one, and is anything but solid ground. I love the quote from the infamous book by A. Huxley titled, *Brave New World*.

> Yes; but what sort of science?" asked Mustapha Mond sarcastically. "You've had no scientific training, so you can't judge. I was a pretty good physicist in my time. Too good–good enough to realize that all our science is just a cookery book, with an orthodox theory of cooking that nobody's allowed to question, and a list of recipes that mustn't be added to except by special permission from the head cook. I'm the head cook now.

So why won't porn go away? We would need to have the "chief cooks" of the scientific community come out and say that evolution is a theory and not fact. That evolution should be taught as metaphysics and not science. The implications of this would be radical! What about the years of saying this was fact and the many museums that have been set up to propagate it, if indeed it was all a mistake. The moral implication would be just as impactful. People would look to another reason why they have the capacity to have sex and think about what is its purpose.

So many in this world pursue happiness and pleasure from sex and yet are most empty of happiness and pleasure. The teaching of evolution has left them bankrupt as a well that has no water.

Top Video Porn Producers	
Country	**Major Producers**
1. 1. United States	Vivid Entertainment, Hustler, Playboy, Wicked Pictures, Red Light District
2. Brazil	Frenesi Films, Pau Brazil, MarcoStudio
3. The Netherlands	Erostream, Midhold Media, Your Choice, Seventeen
4. Spain	Private Media Group, Woodman Entertainment
5. Japan	Soft on Demand, Moodyz
6. Russia	Beate Uhse, SP-Company, Dolphin Entertainment
7. Germany	Trimax, SG-Video, GGG, VideoRama, Zip Production
8. United Kingdom	Hot Rod Productions, JoyBear Pictures, Blue Juice TV, Rude Britannia, Fresh SX
9. Canada	Wild Rose Productions, Eromodel Group, Dugmor
10. Australia	Pistol Media
Other Notables	
Sweden	Maxs Video
Italy	Adamo Entertainment
Denmark	Color Climax Corporation

Country	Studios
France	Euro Choc, Eil du Cochon, Ragtime, Video Marc Dorce, JTC Video, Colmax, Cadinot
Switzerland	Gordi Films, Ikarus
Belgium	GM Videos
Romania	Floyd-Agency
Portugal	Natural Video
Israel	Sex Style
Serbia	Hexor
Czech-Republic	Lupus Pictures, Bel Ami

Porn Revenue from around the globe			
Country	Revenue (Billions)	Per Capita	Notes
China	$27.40	$27.41	1
South Korea	$25.73	$526.76	
Japan	$19.98	$156.75	
US	$13.33	$44.67	
Australia	$2.00	$98.70	
UK	$1.97	$31.84	
Italy	$1.40	$24.08	
Canada	$1.00	$30.21	
Philippines	$1.00	$11.18	
Taiwan	$1.00	$43.41	1
Germany	$0.64	$7.77	1
Finland	$0.60	$114.70	1
Czech Republic	$0.46	$44.94	1

Russia	$0.25	$1.76	1
Netherlands	$0.20	$12.13	
Brazil	$0.10	$53.17	1
Other 212	Unavailable		2
	$97.06 Billion		

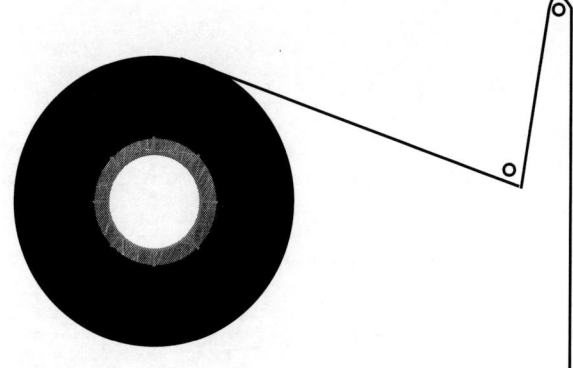

A WAY THAT SEEMS RIGHT

> How long will you love delusions and seek false gods?
> Psalm 4:2 (NIV)

Proverbs says that there is a way that seems right to a man, but in the end it leads to destruction. In the last chapter, I showed that a reason for the progression of porn is that it

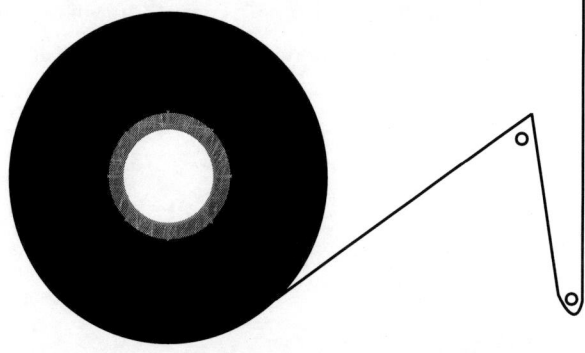

is financially profitable. Not only that, but there is a cultural shift that would need to take place of earthquake level proportions in two areas. One is the way women view their worth or value in today's society and two, a change in the current scientific community. Though these are in my opinion two major players in how porn progresses today, they are not the only two. I believe this chapter piggy backs a bit on the first of these two cultural shifts, specifically our value being in pleasure seeking. Our day is one of dating sites, plastic surgery of every kind, multiple sex partners, and a million ways to find pleasure, yet for what end? For pleasure seeking? But In this chapter I would like to ask is this pursuit of pleasure really satisfying? And this will answer the question from the last chapter of why I believe it is a false pursuit or another way to put it, a non-satisfying pursuit. It is non-satisfying because this pleasure does not last, by being sought out repeatedly. This value in porn pleasure cannot last or satisfy completely. In this chapter I hope to show quite the opposite true. False pursuits of pleasure will not only not satisfy, but will bring a person into extreme un-pleasure in time. Thus this proving that seeing the value of a person in their ability to pursue porn pleasure is a trip to no lasting pleasure at all, but becomes a road to extreme emptiness.

Growing up I would have thought that the chief end of man was to pursue this porn pleasure, for it looked like everyone I was around was benefiting from it. This pleasure seemed to be the means to gaining quite a happy life. But what we didn't know was the destruction that this porn influence was having, not only on us, but on the porn participants themselves.

FINDING OUR PLEASURE IN ANOTHER

Why would anyone desire to view someone else having sex for pleasure? And it's not just watching people having sex because people don't want to watch just anyone having sex, but the right kind of people having sex. These are questions that are answered by psychologists of our day, of which I am not. I am a pastor and teacher of the Bible. The Bible is filled with warnings against lusting after beautiful women. I recall when the Israelites were looking to possess the promised land and a king named Balak from an enemy nation hired a prophet named Balaam to curse the people of Israel. To make a long story short, Balaam could not curse the people, so instead he let the king know how he could defeat them. It was the king's women. Send the women, and they'll intermarry and forget the things of the Lord. The king sent the women, and the rest is Israel's history. Like so many in the past, we have done the same thing. What seemed to be of great value and pleasurable (the women), were really a downfall to the people of Israel. It was not to their gain to find worth in the passing pleasure of the Moabite women, but to their future destruction. How many in our day have experienced this same story. Instead of looking to what really is of value we have sought value in another, though it is temporarily pleasurable, seemingly good and beneficial, but not without its price.

THERE IS NOTHING NEW UNDER THE SUN

Upon reading the Bible when I was seventeen, I did not know where to begin (I was unchurched), so I started at the beginning. The book of Genesis says, "In the beginning God created the heavens and the earth," and so my journey into the world of the Bible began. Now my world was rocked when I came to Genesis 38. There was this story of Onan, who was supposed to have sex with his brother's wife. Man, that sounded pretty pornographic to me. I was excited to read on, and I was not disappointed. Now there is a reason why Onan was supposed to "go into" his brother's wife, but I am not here to explain that but wish you would explore the Levirate law on your own. But to continue with the story, Onan did have sex with her. But what blew me away, being such the porn brain that I was, was that I read that Onan "spilled his seed on the ground!" Oh, man, there it is. The version I read actually said that he spilled his semen on the ground. *That's hardcore porn*, I thought. From that point on, the Bible was fascinating to me. All my preconceived ideas of it were utterly shattered like a piece of pottery thrown against a stone wall.

Every time the Bible said, "and they begat" or "he went into her," my brain raced to thoughts of sex. Images flooded to my brain of what I had seen. So it was, through the lens of porn, that I became a diligent reader of the Bible.

Another incredible passage that has rocked my world is in the book of Ezekiel, chapter 23. This is an allegory of the nation of Israel as seen in the story of two sisters that fall into porn-movie behavior. One sister represents the northern kingdom of Israel while the other represents the southern. The imagery is something straight from a nasty book: "Their breast were there embraced; Their virgin bosom was there pressed." Now that's putting it nicely.

Remembering porn mags and movies as a kid, I could imagine just what God was referring to in this passage. The Scripture goes on and describes the pursuit of more and more sex. "And she lusted for her lovers, the neighboring Assyrians, who were clothed in purple [riches], Captains and rulers, all of the desirable young men, horsemen riding on horses [strong guys]. Thus she committed her harlotry with them, All of them choice men of Assyria and with all for whom she lusted." Porn stars (guys and girls) have gone the distance to look beautiful. Hair coloring, diets, work-out supplements, implants, enhancements, makeup, and much more, all for the pursuit of happiness through pleasure.

So many porn movies in a way mimic the descriptions of these two women in this chapter of the Bible. Not only is there so much lust for more and more, yet never really being satisfied—hence the pursuit of more sex—the women in the allegory, starting at verse nine, seem to fall so short of the desired payoff in their pursuit for more enjoyable sex. "They uncovered her nakedness [shame], took away her sons and daughters [stripping of what is most valuable], and slew her with the sword [death], and she became a byword among women, for they had executed judgment on her."

Oh, the stories are endless of the porn industry's women and men that have pursued happiness through the pursuit of sex and have found the payoff to be of extreme consequence, some even to the point of death.

The all-too-typical story is seen in porn's most current famous woman Jenna Jameson, a story recorded in her bestselling autobiography (that's right, bestselling) called *How to Make Love Like a Porn Star*, published by HarperCollins.

> Determined to overcome this past, Jenna rebounded in the adult-film business, where she encountered sadistic directors, experienced lovers of both sexes, amorous celebrities (from Howard Stern to Marilyn Manson to Tommy Lee), bitter rival starlets, and finally, glory, as she went on to become the biggest porn star the world has ever seen. But her struggle for happiness did not end when the accolades began. For years she wrestled with her resentment at her estranged father, the loneliness of growing up from the age of two without a mother, and her enduring childhood desire to find a man who could give her the security and love she never had.

Though some in the porn industry have become rich, what has been the price? For some it was death; for others it's been massive trauma from what they have been involved in. For others, it's disease from engaging in unprotected sex. But I think for all involved, even the most famous of porn stars that have reached the plateau of excellence in their art, they are known as a byword—*whore*. Now today, that is definitely not as bad as it was years ago, when sex was seen as a means for procreating and not the pursuit of pleasure and happiness. But still, what woman wants to marry a man that is involved with other women? Just think if I came home from an awesome honeymoon with my wife, only to tell her that tomorrow I would be going out with my friends to the strip club and then to have sex with some women, but I'll be back in the morning for breakfast. It devalues the special place that sex is supposed to have in me and my wife's marriage. That's why the Bible says, "Keep the marriage bed honorable" (Heb 13:4). It is to be seen as a place of honor, a special act for us. Porn men and women do not share that honor. One famous porn stud I saw in a thirty-minute show on the porn industry had a wife and a "sidekick" who also lived or hung around the house. I would imagine that many of these end in divorce. Others can't get married because of their job. Most can't even have a "normal" relationship due to their continuing in a constant pursuit of sex. It can't last because it's the wrong pursuit of pleasure. How do we know its wrong? It doesn't satisfy completely. There needs to be a continual pursuit of more and more.

Now back to our allegory of the people of Israel.

For those that look at porn, we have pursued pleasure and satisfaction from watching those that are not satisfied themselves, therefore we can never be satisfied from viewing sex. Verse fourteen says, "She looked at men portrayed on the wall, images of Chaldeans portrayed in vermilion [red]." Here you see the addiction of porn. How many images have we seen, yet is it ever enough? Just when you get done watching one movie, you have to find another, then another. Always looking for something to satisfy, yet never finding it. What's wrong with watching porn? It's addictive. It becomes so addicting that the pursuit of pleasure no longer seems to be the reason anymore, but for some, a pursuit of survival. I'll explain.

LIVING OR LYING

It amazes me to read about the lives of porn stars and hear their stories. They're like the VH1 stories of the rock stars: bad relationship with parents, especially the father, then they were raped or had early sexual experiences (my wife can relate to this), then they were mixed up with a rebellious kind of crowd, went to a party, got hooked up with a "modeling" agency, and a porn actress was born. So many have seen the porn industry as a means to gain something, but not pleasure, because for so many women, there is no pleasure in having sex with twenty guys in a day's work. It becomes survival for them. A way to pay the pills and bills. And for those in their houses watching, it becomes the same after many years of pursuing pleasure from it. Most of the addicted person's time is spent figuring out when they will view porn next, what movie they will watch, whether or not they deleted their browsing history after being on the internet, whether they left any tracks behind. (By the way, browsers today are being made with what is called *porn mode*. It's a feature in the browser that will automatically erase any browsing history.) Survival to the porn viewer is manipulating life to continuing pursuing false pleasure though it gets harder and harder with time. So in both situations, the participant who makes the sex act or the one that sees it, it becomes survival to earn a living or survival to maintain a hidden lifestyle. Pleasure is replaced by extreme work to continue living or lying.

FROM PLEASURE TO BONDAGE

Jesus said the eye is the lamp to the body. There is a radical consequence to viewing porn or engaging in it too. I think this is seen in our next verse we will see in Ezekiel 23. "For she lusted for her illicit lovers, whose flesh is like the flesh of donkeys, and whose issue is like the issue of horses, thus you called to remembrance the lewdness of your youth." 23:20 Wow! Did you catch that? Yes, this is in the Bible you can pick up anywhere and not some obscure Bible from some *Alice in Wonderland* cult group. For the porn actress, she could find another job to earn a living, yet she continues to survive by having sex. And for the person secretly viewing porn, they are under the illusion that their life will crumble if someone finds out about their addiction, when they could actually gain so much from bringing their pursuit of false pleasure into the light. For the porn actress or actor and the person secretly viewing, their lust continues and continues until it becomes something that is absolutely horrid. How many times have I heard people say that they can't believe what they were looking at? I have also heard that women in the porn industry have made decisions to be lesbians on film and off due to the abuse they received from men in the industry. And I can believe that. Though I never have been on a porn set, I have seen enough in life to know that men will go to any length to outdo one another in depravity and desecration of the sacred. This pursuit of false pleasure has always been justified by the ability to be under control, yet for the two people engaged in it, one on the screen and the other in front of a computer or TV, control is lost with time, and abuse of shocking proportions commences. "For she lusted for her illicit lovers, whose flesh is like the flesh of donkeys, and whose issue is like the issue of horses" (NKJV).

There is a way that seems right (and pleasurable), yet it leads to destruction (with the illusion of being in control)

The extremely visual book of Ezekiel goes into imagery of the people's sins with lusting after women. Jesus said that if we lust after women, then adultery is at the door. And Paul the apostle tells us to flee youthful lust which war against the soul.

I think the Bible would make it clear that lust leads to something that is not a desired result. Just like when I was a teenager in the backyard of a party drinking a beer, I didn't think to myself, "Hey I want to be a drop down drunk one day." There was excitement (pleasure) in the backyard with the friends in the Valley. So lust has a desired effect that is excitement. I don't think anyone has grand dreams of being addicted to images as an adult. I am a mentor for many men in all parts of the world who never thought that this would happen to them. For some, their viewing images has progressed to multiple partner relationships. For all of them, porn has become a life dominating bondage. To me, that means the behavior of viewing porn has become first on their minds, and all decisions made are brought before the idol of porn as to not upset the god they serve. Some might not understand that. I actually hope that you don't understand it. That would mean that you have not experienced the addiction.

Addiction defined is as "the condition of being habitually or compulsively occupied with or involved in something."[22]

FINANCIAL SUCCESS DOESN'T MEAN YOU ARE NOT IN BONDAGE!

I would add that it is a behavior of a certain kind that falls into addiction. If someone is addicted in helping people, I don't think many books would be written about that person's addiction as being a problem. Addiction, as our culture looks at it, is a habitual or compulsive behavior that leads to a person's destruction. Porn is bad because it is a habitual behavior that leads to destruction. That might sound weird to some, and for those that make a lot of money from the industry it would seem ridiculous. They have money in the bank and a good reputation in the business community. How could that be bad? And as Paul said in his letter to Corinth, if there is no resurrection from the dead then eat, drink, and be merry, for tomorrow we die. But if this is not the case, and the man from Nazareth rose from the dead in conquering death, then a real problem exists. "What does it profit for a man to gain the whole world yet lose his soul?" (Luke 9:25). So what might, in a secular sense, seem successful, in another sense is not. Perspective or better yet, revelation is everything.

Not everyone in the porn industry is romantically involved due to the pursuit of false pleasure of sex. Obviously as stated, there is the financial gain associated with the business of porn. But we should not judge success by monetary gain, for this will not satisfy either. There are endless stories of women that have gone through tragic upbringings and have found porn as a means of financial gain which has brought temporary satisfaction to their lives. For more and more this seems to be a vocation now, as I have shown by one article titled, "Mommy, I want to be a Porn Star." Even pre-teens look up to a successful porn star. The industry paints a picture of successful porn stars being like athletes or models. They seem to have it all, but for many it is not like this. Let's ask the question, Why are they then involved in the industry participating in such actions? It's because of money if not the pleasure of sex. If there were no payment, would they be doing it? Having sex for money is called prostitution, and no one would presume that paying for a prostitute is engaging in a relationship of lasting significance and completely satisfying. Sorry, but the *Pretty Woman* movie is not the norm. Pleasure for sex is set aside for pleasure of money. And this is still placing value in something that cannot satisfy completely. Sure the world is gained, but there is an incredible loss.

THE MIND OF A PORN ADDICT AND ITS IMPACT ON THE FAMILY

For the addict, love for porn is above the love of family and friends. When making a decision about whether to go out with the wife or stay home by themselves, the addict will choose to stay alone at the house to spend time with his friend, the porn images. Even if he goes out with his wife, his mind is so polluted that he thinks that this will give him "brownie points" for future time to be alone with his god. I know that sounds so deceptive and it is. But this is a typical statement from some of the men that I mentor: "I look at porn online and act out in the morning, at noon, and in the evening. I neglect everything else that I should be doing. I just got divorced last week—marriage failed in part due to this issue."

Obviously in my own mind I have had these thoughts, and so I share them with you. The addict's number one goal in life is to have undivided time with his images. Nothing can get in the way, and nothing will unless there is a dethroning of this god. This is how all those who have had addictions have thought. This is bad and not good. Instead of building up relationships with our wives, kids, and friends, we have put images of women or men having sex before them, and this is a bad decision that results in more bad decisions, so much so that before you know it, you have a bad marriage and your kids, and friends don't like you anymore. Look at how many divorces are now influenced by adultery and porn. It's a new era in the divorce industry where cheap divorce is sold on the internet. One internet site boasts its company's productivity in this area by saying this: "Complete Your Divorce Online: Over a Quarter of One Million Users to Date!"

Porn is placing a role in people's lives more today than any other in the U.S. I don't need to go into how a woman gets crushed when finding out her man is addicted to porn. But it is not good. Still, people might say, "Why is it not good?" But let's take porn addiction to its conclusion. A man views porn and it becomes a habitual behavior that plays a role in all his decisions in life. He spends his money on it and would rather be viewing porn then spending time with his family. Ah, the family! There it is. This is what is damaged when in bondage to porn. The family! If a family is torn apart on the small scale, then our society is torn apart on the large scale. If it's okay for men and women to view porn, then maybe there will be no more need for physical sex. The addicted person is happier in the self-gratification than a real physical relationship anyway. If porn is good, then we are saying it's okay for a parent to put their child in a room to watch TV while we, with joy, go to our computers to drink deep of porn worship. I'm trying to help us understand that saying *yes* to porn is saying *no* to those that we are to love intimately. And without that love, consequently we have a society of delinquent children and divorce (sound familiar?). If this is the case, then Huxley was correct in his infamous book *A Brave New World*. There is no need for sex or family. The state can run them both. If loving relationships in life are not seen as of infinite worth and value, then there is no reason to see porn as a threat.

Now as a pastor and someone who claims that Christ is of infinite value and a treasure, there is even more about this issue. Why should we see the family as of any value at all? We live in an interesting time. Technology has made progress so fast, like spoken of by the prophet Daniel, who said at the end of his book, "Knowledge will increase more and more" (Daniel 12:4). With these steps in technology, the traditional ancient family is under more attack than ever before. We don't even need a dad anymore (hence the war of redefining marriage). We can marry a tree for goodness' sake and still have kids. Artificial insemination has made this possible. So why do we need a family anyway? What is the point? This is where we are in our culture. This really needs to be asked because it's the direction we are going. Does it benefit my kids that I am around showing them how to treat a woman (my wife) or how to treat them? Can't they get that from anyone? And if they don't need to be in a relationship to have kids, then why is it important for me and my wife to show them a good example of a traditional family? I mean, the traditional family is no longer needed because of technology, right? What does our traditional family contribute to my kids? What's with these entire questions, right (I'm laughing)? I ask these questions to simply state that there is no point to the traditional family if there is no Creator who has revealed his will to us in history and through the person of Jesus of Nazareth. No point. We can say that our culture will go down the toilet or society will be a mess, but who's to say the *A Brave New World* life won't be a happy life filled with pleasure?

CONCLUSION

See, self-happiness is what our culture says is numero uno in life. It's about me, my happiness. Porn is good because it makes me happy; I like it. I make money off it. See the nice house I have and the respect in the business community. Look at my rewards. I'm happy. Okay, but what's the problem with this? One big thing. Addiction does not make anyone happy! It's interesting that on TV there are countless reality TV shows that demonstrate this. Flavor Flav from Public Enemy is there with a bunch of actors and musicians that are addicted to something. They don't seem too fulfilled. Not much happiness going on. Rich, rich people don't seem too happy. They're always stressed about their cash. So when the porn star justifies her work as good because of her success, I don't buy it. It's not lasting or satisfying. Why would a porn actress stop doing porn if it's so satisfying? We can convince ourselves otherwise in order to live with ourselves, but honestly, it is not.

Saying no only makes sense if you believe that your family and loved ones' relationships are of more value and worth. This can only happen in my opinion (and I do have good company) from looking at what Jesus says about family and relationships. If you think you are smarter than Jesus, then anything I say or really have said is of no use to you. You have placed infinite value on your comfort in nonsatisfying pleasure. Shallow is that well, and a road most traveled.

The reason this is so important is that in visiting those dying in the hospital over the past fifteen years, I have never had one person ask about their money, house, car, or any other nonliving thing. The questions always revolve around people—their loved ones. They wish they invested more in people.

In the end, death awaits, and the unknown will now become reality. Porn at that time is meaningless and a waste of time and a painful memory of choosing mud instead of a wonderful tall glass of water.

We are half-hearted creatures,
fooling about with drink and sex and
ambition when infinite joy is offered us,
like an ignorant child who wants to go on
making mud pies in a slum because he
cannot imagine what is meant by the offer
of a holiday at the sea. We are far too easily pleased.
—C.S. Lewis, *The Weight of Glory*

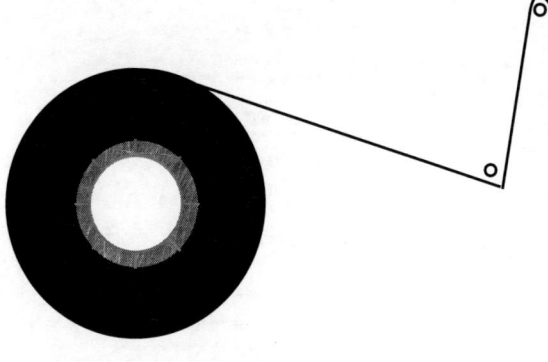

THE CHRISTIAN COMMUNITY

> Oh, Taste and see that the Lord is good!
> Psalm 34:8 (NKJV)

Sex and Christianity seem to never go hand in hand. Or if you do hear of the two terms together, more than likely it has to do with a scandal of sorts. Yet what does the Bible teach?

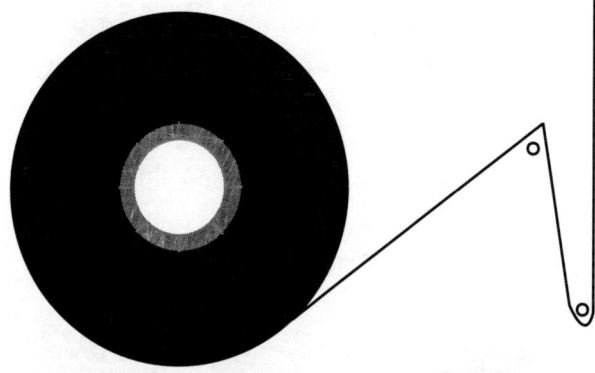

A whole book of the Bible is given over to the idea of passion in an intimate relationship between a man and a woman. Song of Solomon is quite a cool book with fondling fruits galore! But it's not talking about fruit on a tree, but the passion of a sexual relationship with someone you see of worth. I'm so glad that book is included in the Jewish writing of the Old Testament. It agrees with the rest of Holy Scripture that sex is something to be enjoyed and treasured. Yes, that's right! Sex is something to be enjoyed and treasured between a husband and a wife. The Bible does set that parameter: a husband and wife and not any other sexual relation. But within that marriage there is to be a passion for one another like no other.

SEX A GIFT FROM GOD, TO HIS GLORY

Why is sex in marriage supposed to be enjoyed and treasured? Because it is a gift from the Almighty, a part of his grace in our life to glorify himself. My wife is a gift from God. And we are told to delight in the Lord. At his right hand are pleasures. He does whatever pleases him we are told in Psalm 115:3. You get that? God is pleased by me enjoying his gifts. I do not seek the gift itself, but him through the gift! I see my wife as a gift, as I have stated. I pursue the pleasure of the Lord in pleasure with my wife. As Christians, we are to be joyful of all of God's graces. Why? Because they are from him! Be a cheerful giver. Don't just give money to something, but give it cheerfully. Meaning it's important that we find joy in giving. So the action of giving is not the goal but doing it with joy! How can we do that? We do that because in God's presence, there is fullness of joy. If we are pursuing God in our giving, then joy will accompany the gift.

In the book of Philippians, Paul says that suffering has been granted to the church! It's a gift from the Lord! That's how Paul could have joy in the midst of suffering. He saw it as a gift from God in exalting the suffering of Christ through his own suffering, and to Paul that was awesome, and he was thankful that God would use his life to exalt Christ whether in good times or hard. Gifts of God are to be cherished, whether in the form of a bride or suffering. Both come from God.

The Christian community seems to be lacking pleasure in marriages. I have had counseling encounters with Christian couples that have not had sex more than three times a year! That's insane if it's true. We have somehow got to a place of thinking the pursuit of pleasure in the Christian life is wrong. And so who would want to have a Christian marriage when they appear so boring, where sex is all about procreation and seems about as pleasurable as doing roof work in the 115-degree Tucson, Arizona summer! "Let's get the job done as quick as possible!" It seems that sex is a duty in the Christian's life not to be desired and especially not a pursuit of God. This is not the kind of relationship that a Christian should have with his wife, let alone God. We enjoy God. We are Christians not because of duty only, but because he is pleasurable and to be enjoyed.

We can, though, pursue God in the midst of a passionate sexual relationship with our spouses, and it would be dishonoring to God to think otherwise. God's gifts are to be cherished and enjoyed for they come from him!

> Drink water from your own cistern,
> And running water from your own well.
> Should your fountains be dispersed abroad?
> Streams of water in the streets?
> Let them be only your own,
> And not for strangers with you.
> Let your fountain be blessed,
> And rejoice with the wife of your youth.
> As a loving deer and a graceful doe,
> Let her breasts satisfy you at all times;
> And always be enraptured with her love.
> Proverbs 5:15–19 (NKJV)

Enjoying your spouse is not an option; it is commanded. "Rejoice with the wife of your youth!"

Ask in my name that your joy may be complete. Jesus tells his disciples in John 16:24 that it is a great thing to come to the Father in his name that we may receive from him, so we may experience joy! "Do not deprive one another except for a time." Paul says this in his letter to the church in 1st Corinthians 7:5. Why not deprive one another? He goes on, "So that you are not tempted." Don't deprive each other of the gift you are to one another. Why? Because the gift is from God, and God opens his arms and satisfies the desires of every living thing (Psalm 145:16), and that there is pleasure in drinking from the river of life (Psalm 36:8). We experience God's grace (undeserved gift) within the sexual relation as we seek to please and be pleased by one another.

It is wonderful to know that you are a gift of God for your spouse. God accomplishes his wonderful purpose in my wife through His work in me. To put it another way, I become an instrument of the Almighty in giving wonderful pleasure to my wife. Being a part of God's plan in blessing people is such a joy.

DUTY NOT JOY IN CHRISTIAN MARRIAGE

So what kind of joy is there in the Christian community's marriages? I'm sure you see a passion like no other to be desired and cherished, right?

We see divorce in the Christian world on par with the secular world—no difference! I have had countless meetings with couples in the church environment that reflect the lack of seeing sex in marriage as a gift from God to be sought and pursued. I remember my wife and I attending a Christian marriage conference, and it was the time to talk about sex. The room was quiet, and the husband and wife leaders started in. The wife started by telling us about their sexual arrangements, which to me and my wife seemed a bit interesting. I had never heard of a sexual arrangement before, in the church that is. Then the lady began to talk about how she gave him sex, and he gave her money to shop. I thought to myself, *I think that is prostitution.* Where is the joy or passion in pursuing God in the midst of his gift (spouse)? How can sex not be seen as passionate? Why is it seen that way in this community of those that are supposed to be followers of the Christ whose last day's are called "the Passion." Aren't we to be the most passionate people on the earth?

I wish this was not the norm, but I fear it is.

"Marriage is honorable among all, and the bed undefiled." (Heb 13:4, NKJV) Yet it is. Even in my own brain I have had this tidal wave of nonpassionate teaching come my way and think, *Okay, I'm supposed to have sex with my wife. It's my duty!* The world looks at Christian marriage and get's the idea that we are not into the commitment as well. When we see a Christian couple portrayed on the TV, it usually looks quite boring, and anything but pleasurable. The Christian culture has a default way of thinking. In light of this thinking, many pursue pleasure in those that are not the gift, not from the hand of God. This biblically is the wrong pursuit of pleasure because it is not from the hand of God by exalting his Word, and so will lead to addiction, bondage, and destruction. But so many are in this situation. They do not pursue God in the midst of serving their wives sexually, so they pursue pleasure in the nonsacred—porn—which leads them to divorce. So many divorces today; more and more are seeing porn play a role in it.

> The Internet was a significant factor in 2 out of 3 divorces (American Academy of Matrimonial Lawyers in 2003 - divorcewizards.com).
>
> 47 percent of families said pornography is a problem in their home (Focus on the Family Poll, October 1, 2003).[23]

JUDGMENT BEGINS IN THE HOUSE OF GOD

It's amazing how the stats in the U.S. say that we are a Christian nation. Yet by our decisions we prove otherwise, or at least they show that the church is struggling with coming "out from among them" (I Corinthians 6:17). If you don't want porn, then stop viewing it! We love to bag on the world, don't we? How influenced is the church when it comes to porn?

Here are some insightful statistics about Christians, pastors, and church pornography:

> A 1996 Promise Keepers survey at one of their stadium events revealed that over 50% of the men in attendance were involved with pornography within one week of attending the event.
>
> 51% of pastors say cyber-porn is a possible temptation. 37% say it is a current struggle (Christianity Today, Leadership Survey, 12/2001).
>
> Over half of evangelical pastors admit viewing pornography last year.
>
> Roger Charman of Focus on the Family's Pastoral Ministries reports that approximately 20 percent of the calls received on their Pastoral Care Line are for help with issues such as pornography and compulsive sexual behavior.
>
> In a Christianity Today survey taken in 2000, 33% of clergy admitted to having visited a sexually explicit Web site. Of those who had visited a porn site, 53% had visited such sites "a few times" in the past year, and 18% visit sexually explicit sites between a couple of times a month and more than once a week.

> 29% of born again adults in the U.S. feel it is morally acceptable to view movies with explicit sexual behavior (The Barna Group).
>
> 57% of pastors say that addiction to pornography is the most sexually damaging issue to their congregation (Christians and Sex Leadership Journal Survey, March 2005).

Statistics on women with pornography addiction:

> 28% of those admitting to sexual addiction are women (internet-filter-review.com).
>
> 34% of female readers of Today's Christian Woman's online newsletter admitted to intentionally accessing Internet porn in a recent poll and 1 out of every 6 women, including Christians, struggles with an addiction to pornography (Today's Christian Woman, Fall 2003).[24]

This to me says it all. Who do we need to be preaching to? The first answer is me! If I don't see the empty well that porn is, I will continue to go back and try filling my bucket over and over. Second, it has to be the church. Pastors and teachers need to not shy away from teaching the whole Bible. This is my job. As I have previously pointed out, the Bible is loaded with the issue of porn and pleasure.

When I began reading the Bible at the age of seventeen, I was a senior in High school. I remember coming across the passage I referred to in an earlier chapter from the book of Genesis chapter 38 that was so sexually graphic, I had to tell someone. That week in school I had it in my mind to approach all the vocal Christians I knew to see if they knew about the character named Onan from the Genesis chapter. To my surprise, they all had no clue what I was referring about. Some even denied that the story was in the Bible. This was my first lesson about Christians and the culture. Not all who say they are Christians know what is in their Bible. Why was it this way? Why was it that these church kids in High School, who were raised in the Bible, did not know the stories of the false pursuits of pleasure? There are so many. In fact, every story in the Bible in some way is purposed to show that God is a better pleasure than the false pleasure of this world. Obviously their parents and pastors did not find it important to share with them that particular story. Today I realize that a failure has happened in the church due to me (and others) not living right in my own pursuit of pleasure. Judgment begins in the house of God, and that's me.

GOD JUDGES THOSE OUTSIDE THE CHURCH!

Paul, in the book of 1 Corinthians 5, deals with a man who is having sex with his dad's wife. The church seems to be tolerant of this man to Paul's disappointment. Paul then says to the church at Corinth, "When I told you not to keep company with anyone who is sexually immoral... I did not mean those outside the church, but do not even eat with one named a 'brother' who is sexually immoral" (I Corinthians 5:9–11). My point in this scripture is that the church needn't rag on the "Ron Jeremys" of the porn industry. He is not a Christian. (He comes from a Jewish family though!) So it becomes apparent that we are not to stay away from those in the porn industry but try and persuade as to show Christ of more infinite value than the well of porn. To debate the industry influence in the culture can change a country's policy, but still a soul is lost. Those in the church are told not to keep company with those in the church that will not repent (have a change of mind) about their sexual immorality. This again is a sad fact of our church culture. Most people who call themselves Christians do not in the slightest feel grieved for staying up late viewing porn while their families sleep. I have even seen a situation where a "Christian" husband and wife are so blinded to the things of God that they would rather have a swingers' marriage than divorce. I could depress you with the countless situations where adultery has been committed and the person remained unrepentant while the church family around them lay powerless in their tolerance through fear of offending. If the church were worried about pornography, then we would have a whole lot more church discipline going on, but instead we have homosexual pastors and priests, friendly churches, happy people, and seeker sensitivity (whatever that means). Paul saw that the church at Corinth loved to debate who was the greatest pastor or what were the greatest gifts of the Holy Spirit (i.e. who could speak in tongues the most), yet they missed the greatest of all: a love for Christ that is uncompromising.

I was reading Ron Jeremy's book titled *The Hardest (Working) Man in Show Business*, and he talks about his fear of death. I thought it to be very relatable. I, too, have had dark nights like that, especially when I was younger, when I would freak myself out thinking about what would happen to me when I died. Haven't we all thought about that at some point. What is the benefit of me judging a man like Ron Jeremy when, as a pastor, I am not able to judge those within the church body to which I am an overseer? Or, what is it for you to judge him when you as a Christian will not tell your Christian friend that what they are doing is unscriptural?

CHANGE MY HEART, O GOD!

From the teaching in the Psalms (and throughout the Holy Scriptures), only God can change a heart. My part is to seek the change. Jesus said, "Seek and you shall find." For those who are spiritually made alive in Christ (I'm speaking Christian-ese now), you have everything that pertains to godliness. Freedom from sin is yours in Jesus. He bought your freedom. Those that are in the porn industry have not sought that freedom; it is not theirs. The Bible gives us strong illustrations about a person who is not born of the spirit. They are dead, blind, a captive, chained, in bondage, poor, hungry, and thirsty. Why do we continue to judge the dead when what they need is life? God will judge those who are outside of the church, Paul says. God will do it, so we don't have to. What does that mean? I believe that means that we are not to act in judgment on the unbeliever as we would with a believer. Our job with the unbeliever is to bring them to an understanding of the treasure Christ is in the hope of eternal pleasures.

The writer of "Amazing Grace," John Newton, was a slave trader, and through the divine grace of God, he became one who sought better, greater, and lasting pleasure in Christ . He had a wonderful tenderness towards the lost as seen in this story:

> A company of travelers fall into a pit: one of them gets a passenger to draw him out. Now he should not be angry with the rest for falling in; nor because they are not yet out, as he is. He did not pull himself out: instead, therefore, of reproaching them, he should show them pity.... A man, truly illuminated, will no more despise others, than Bartimaeus, after his own eyes were opened, would take a stick, and beat every blind man he met.[25]
>
> Psalm 36:8 (NIV)

So the church needs to look at how we are obeying our own Scripture in how we look at the industry. We truly are to hate sin. "I gain understanding from your precepts therefore I hate every wrong path" (Psalm 119:104, NKJV), yet I am to not judge the unbeliever as Paul says, through the inspiration of the Holy Spirit.

Let's get back to the Word on this issue of how we crack the porn industry's influence in our lives. Informed and knowledgeable is a good thing. In this book, I have enjoyed writing about the industry yet knowing that those individuals that move the industry are not Christians, and because of that truth, I am to see them as a field ready for harvesting not a weed for pulling. That is not my prerogative.

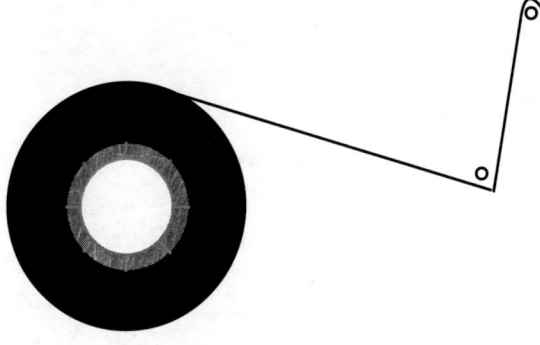

CHANGING THINGS

> God Grant me the serenity to accept the things I
> cannot change, courage to change the things I can,
> and the wisdom to know the difference.
> —Karl Paul Reinhold Niebuhr

I was raised on his prayer from the *American Theologian*.
We live in an era of change. That's the new slogan for the

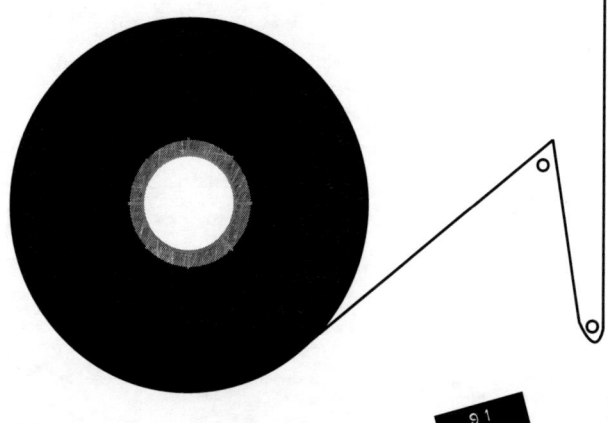

country I assume from this last presidential race. But how to change and what to change is the question in this chapter.

If we want things to change, I believe it will not be through research of the effects of porn on the family or finding scientific standards to prove a biological chemical is released in the brain as in this 2005 article by Jerry Spangler, "Net Porn Called a Threat to Marriage."

> Manning was careful to say that more research needs to be done into the effects of pornography on social relationships, and that cause-and-effect correlations often don't meet scientific review standards. However, she added, ongoing studies are finding a reappearing scientific link—people who have just viewed pornographic images and people who have just been given a powerful narcotic have similar brain chemistry profiles.[26]

The way it changes is not through proving some research but through a heart change, which results in a mind change. We need to think a different way. I speak to those in the Christian community because that's my environment. If we all (and I include myself) change the way we view pleasure, passion, and the pursuit of God in the church through teaching the Bible in its entirety, then my belief is the actions will change. In the church, marriages will become passionate and highly sexual (though I don't need to know about it,), pleasurable, and given in pleasure. This is how God has designed it! Sex could have been unpleasurable, but then again, I go back to the pleasure of God. He is pleasurable, and his gifts are to be desired.

"Delight ourselves in the Lord" He is delightful, and as a gift, so is your partner in marriage.

Do not be conformed to this world but transformed by the renewing of your mind. We need a brain transplant. The reason the porn industry has achieved its success is due to the church's failure to see the pursuit of pleasure in marriage as the pursuit of God. And in this case, changing things will not come from changing a law to restrict porn on the internet or cable TV. This, I think, is a mask for the real need, which is repentance, in the church. James says, "Turn your laughter to mourning," James 4:9 meaning wake up and think about what we have been doing.

So the church first needs a work done in it, and I've spoken to the church in the previous chapter. But I want to spend time for those that are addicted to porn and want out. I know what it is like to feel the pull of addiction. My life of drinking started when I was in kindergarten. My dad had a few friends over partying a bit, and I went to drink of his Budweiser and yuck! It was being used as an ashtray! That took the desire for cigarettes away instantaneously. Beer was a norm for me. Pot was around, and in elementary school, I remember smoking dope from a homemade pipe made from a Coke can. Sexual addiction has always been in my life too. As a child I remember smooching with girls, grabbing their private parts, and just thinking the most violent thoughts in lust. Sex is violence (*Jane's Addiction's* Perry Ferrell said it), and that's biblical too. I dealt treacherously with the girls I was around. I remember being in college, and an old girlfriend came over my house to give me an old letter that I wrote her when I was in junior high school.

Oh man, how embarrassing! It said all kinds of lustful stuff. I don't even remember writing it, but I know that I did. It seems like I was just full of sexual junk from when I was a wee lad. I've known my wife since I was seven. She knows what a little pervert I was and the kind of guys I hung out with. I love those guys, but wow, were we twisted when we were young.

As an early teen, I would spend most of my weekends in the Valley at clubs. The Country Club was a happening spot for metal shows back then. Rat, Warrant, and my favorite, Racer X, were big. At times we would hang out on the Sunset Strip to watch metal shows at The Roxy and The Whisky a Go-Go. But this life just increased my lust for women. I was around older women all the time. Women that were bold sexually and would make a young guy like me blush.

The internet became a safe place to view that which I used to have to go out to find. And like many that read this, porn has found a safe place in your house to grow, until you have reached a place where it has taken over every room in your house. It's become so big that your family has no more space in it! You've tried, and nothing has worked to stop you from going back, as a sheep to the slaughter, as a dog returning to its own vomit!

For so many, damage has been done that is so devastating their lives will never be the same as before. I pray the next things I mention will help you.

A GRACE THAT FREES, TO GOD'S GLORY

Only the power of Christ can truly free us from this addiction properly. Let me explain a bit here. Many people can be rid of porn addiction by other methods than the one I suggest. As I write this, there are plenty of people in sex rehabilitation centers drinking from the well of psychology with the desired result to be freed entirely from porn addiction. I believe this is nothing more than going from one empty bucket to another. You can be free of porn, but now you move to another. Porn addiction creates patterns within our lives in which we desire more and more from one picture to another. The reason a person goes from one addiction to another is because they never drink from a well that can give them what they truly need. My belief is in the words of Jesus of Nazareth who promises that he will satisfy.

So for the nonbeliever, I do believe that you can be free of porn through secular principles, yet no permanent change has taken place but a transfer of similar behavior. This is so common, is it not? One stops drinking or smoking only to get overweight. One stops eating too much only to get addicted to porn. And the beat goes on and on. Similar behavior is moved and then replaced rather than removed, and the latter is what I believe happens to the Christian, by the grace of God.

The permanent change that we seek is one described by Pastor John Piper in a sermon called "Set Free by the Spirit of Life in Christ Jesus."

> I have said many times in years gone by that the

only sin we can defeat is a forgiven sin. Let me say it more carefully this morning: the only sin that you can defeat in daily life and replace with righteousness is a sin forgiven for Christ's sake. I say it carefully because I know there are natural ways to overcome bad habits that aren't based on Christ at all. But when those changes occur in life without forgiveness from Christ, the result is not God's righteousness, but self-righteousness—which in God's eyes is no righteousness. So I say it again and carefully: the only sin that you can defeat in daily life and replace with righteousness is a sin forgiven for Christ's sake.[27]

Addiction in the Bible is called idolatry.

> Put to death, therefore, whatever belongs to your earthly nature: sexual immorality, impurity, lust, evil desires and greed, which is idolatry.
>
> Colossians 3:5 (NKJV)

It is through idolatry that porn becomes of infinite value to the person addicted to it. For a person to get off the porn, they need first to be concerned about God and not themselves. And this, too, is by the grace of God.

Come to think of it, it is the grace of God that teaches us to abstain from worldly lusts (Titus 2:11 NKJV). God's grace is seen in the cross of Christ to save us from the penalty of our sin and the power to make us holy positionally and practically. That's quite a sentence that says, "Without God, it's impossible to be completely free."

Grace is God's unmerited favor given through Jesus in

saving us and the Holy Spirit in making us holy like Jesus. All that I mention from here on as ways to find freedom from porn is a gift to be sought. "I will seek you!" "Seek and you shall find, knock and the door will be opened, ask and you shall receive" (Matthew 7:7). We read in the book of John that it is to our joy that our God answers our cries. "Until now you have not asked anything in my name, ask and it will be given to you that your joy may be complete" (John 16:15, NKJV).

Do you want to be free? Seek these that I mention, as the psalmist says, day and night.

THE GLORY TO GOD

> Not to us but to your name be the glory.
> Psalm 115:1 (NKJV)

Our thoughts need to be directed in the concern for the glory of God. If this is not the case, then failure will be sure to happen. Fear of losing your wife or your job won't cut it. For teens, the fear of being caught by their parents will never overcome the passing pleasure in porn viewing. When concerned about God's glory and name, we experience a different fruit in our griefs for our failure to uphold the glory of God.

And this leads to repentance. What a word. It sounds so…so…churchy, and so it is! The Hebrew Teshuva might sound not so churchy, as it has been around for a long time. "Let us examine our ways and test them, and let us return to the LORD" (Lam 3:40, NIV). I think this is a great example in the Jewish Scriptures about repentance.

It's a turning away and a turning to. It's important to note that it is a gift, one of many graces (gifts) of God, to be sought with a persistence that we see among those that do not believe. Those in secular society seek the worldly items full force, and so the Christian is to seek the Lord's graces in similar manner, yet going after the greater and more satisfying reward. When turning to God, it is understood from the Christian Scriptures that we are turning to God, who is to be viewed as our treasure. When found, we, with joy, sell everything to be with the treasure (Matthew 10:44). So the repentance that God gives is a pursuit of him with joy! Blessed are those that thirst and hunger for God! And the world blessed is happy.

Repentance also carries a fruit. In 2 Corinthians 7, Paul talks about godly sorrow that leads to repentance, but sorrow of the world produces death. What's the difference between godly sorrow and secular sorrow? One has a sorrow directed vertically toward God, and the latter is a horizontal sorrow directed toward mankind. It's important to look at this point for I believe it is the reason the human heart has such a problem with saying, "I'm wrong." When more concerned with my own circumstances than God's glory, I will likely manipulate my wrong or even lie about it for fear of shame before men or my reputation is lost amongst colleagues. That fear of man that brings a snare is so great that saying anything other than, "I'm wrong," will suffice for most situations only to prolong a true change. We have seen countless times on the news where someone, who has blown it, says, "If I have done anything to hurt the family, I am sorry." What? *If?* That just torques us! Change can't happen when fear of man is involved; for man is the living dead that is living yet on the road to death, and serving and being mastered by a dying person will result in death and no change. Worldly sorrow leads to death because it is a sorrow rooted in this fear of those that will die. The imperfect (death) cannot produce the perfect (life). Yet godly sorrow is a sorrow for an offence seen against the perfect that is God. This sorrow doesn't hide wrong due to the fear of man but brings out the wrong because of the perfection of God. God is the Father, and when a child knows the goodness of the father, his desire is to be right with him. His sorrow is productive and is rooted in knowing that the Father is merciful and kind, slow to anger, and rich in love. He can say openly, "I'm wrong" without any fear.

"God's kindness leads you toward repentance" (Romans 2:4).

DRINKING FROM THE RIGHT WELL

Where do you drink from? This book is about us who have drunk from the well of porn and have been left unsatisfied.

The book of John, the fourth chapter, is where we find the right well to drink from. I love this passage. It's quite famous. It's the story of Jesus meeting a Samaritan woman at a well on his way to Jerusalem. Jesus asked for a drink from the woman, to her surprise, and so begins a dialogue between the unsatisfied and the satisfied, the empty and the full. She had six husbands! So this woman is like so many of us who have gone from one excitement to the next, only to come up short and wanting. Think of how many images we, who have viewed porn, have seen—thousands upon thousands, and yet they never seem to be enough. People in sexual addiction go from one fetish to another, always pushing the envelope of "nasty" just a bit more, until we, like this woman, show the signs of a war unwon. We don't know her name, but we could put our names in the story, and it would work just the same. We are no different.

Jesus offers her a new well: him. He continues to tell her that if you continue to drink from this well, you will be thirsty again. And then like Jesus did so often, he invites the women to partake of him. Notice it wasn't a philosophy that he was asking her to write out and study, but it was a call to trust in him, the God/man.

Now how do you partake in Jesus? Simply put, it's by trusting his Word. "My Word is truth," he declared. I trust that the Lord will satisfy more than porn. I seek him as I would the porn that I sought. I think of him instead of thinking of another time I can be alone to view porn. In essence, I worship him and find wonderful delight and joy in him for he is our treasure and great reward. So many look to the Lord yet do it without any joy or delight. An American pastor, John Piper, said, "He is not worshiped where he is not enjoyed and treasured." And I tend to agree wholeheartedly. When I was into porn, I did it wholeheartedly and thought about it continually. It brought me happiness. Doesn't that sound weird? But if there was not any pleasure in it, then no one would progress further in it. For as the young and famous mathematician Pascal once wrote, "Happiness is the end all of everyone, even those that hang themselves." I find this woman is somewhat caught in an ancient quandary. So many of us consistently think that we will find fulfillment in a sexual relationship. Sure, it doesn't have to be sexual, but I'm talking about the influence of porn, jumping from one image to another. Like the sexual satisfaction will be enough for us. People get married in thinking that their marriage partners make them complete. If that is your thinking, then you, like me, are right here with this woman, drinking from the wrong well. "How long will you love worthlessness and seek falsehood?" Psalm 4:2 (NKJV). This can sound so foreign to us, for my generation was spoon-fed on the idea that the more gratification the better. This is what King David wrote in Psalm 73:25 (NKJV):

> "Whom have I in heaven but You?
> And there is none upon earth that I desire besides You."

This fits well with what Jesus said. He alone can satisfy completely, eternally (not temporally). Our partners will fail us in so many ways no doubt. If you make your partner your god, you will be utterly disappointed and betrayed, for they cannot bear that burden; they never were intended to do so.

ACCOUNTABILITY

Porn addiction is synonymous with darkness. The clubs I went to with friends were dark. Vegas is only cool at night,. There is something to be said about doing deeds of darkness in darkness, for the light seems to quench its power.

Accountability is about bringing the addiction into the light. I remember the old vampire flicks from Elvira, the mistress of the dark. I thought they were so spooky. The scenes were in creepy-looking houses that were ancient. Who in their right mind would want to watch a scary flick like that in the day? That messes the whole thing up.

Light tends to spoil the darkness and make the darkness seem less intimidating and strong. So it is with porn. Most people that I've known who have been into porn have not been into it in a congregational setting; it's a private affair. Usually it's done in a dark room or at nighttime when everyone is asleep. It's just the person and a computer or a TV, a few extra items that we need not go into, and tada! That's it! And I don't see many windows or doors for that matter in adult stores. Porn people like their privacy. So the environment of a porn addict is one of being alone or at least hidden from others. Bringing the addiction into the open doesn't just seem to kill the strength of the sin, but it actually does do it by no longer keeping the consistent environment of secrecy in which the addiction thrives.

Accountability not only means bringing the addiction into the "light," but it also entails a continual, honest, and growing relationship with a person that has freed himself from porn. Many people who have not been into porn do not have the understanding of the sick, wicked, and deceptive minds that they are working with. Porn addicts want to be alone with their porn. Their thinking is always to pursue more porn. My dad used to say, "You can't BS an old BSer." And in that crude statement, I believe there is a truth.

And now I will give you an idea of the porn person's

mind. If you put a filter on the computer, we will find a way around it by doing picture searches on Google using words like *blonde*, *European*, or a random girl's name. We know how to get inside search engine preferences to ensure that we will have the best possible chance of finding the gold on the other side of the rainbow. If that doesn't work, we look into peer-to-peer software that is on third party sites to download so the filter doesn't recognize that porn is being accessed. And the heart can be so wicked that it will lie to a spouse to get the password of the filter software. The lust for porn knows no bounds.

With what I just said, now I wish to show that accountability with a freed porn addict is the real but not the ideal! It would be ideal if everyone in the Christian church could minister to a porn addict. If only all of us in the church knew the depth of our sins and the wickedness of our minds. But so many in the body see themselves as "not as bad off" as the porn addict or any other kind of addict. *Sure I might sin a bit*, someone might think to himself, but the biblical reality is any type of missing the mark of God's perfection and glory is an offence to him, and, because of such action on our part, the cross was needed. Jesus' blood was shed for the porn addict and the prideful pomp. Who did Christ come for anyway? Was it not for the sinner? Yes it was! "Christ Jesus came into the world to save sinners" I Timothy 1:15. There are church leaders who dare not or do not know how to minister to one in bondage, because they do not understand their own measure of wickedness. Jesus was the master teacher, incredible in tenderness towards the ignorant and humble, yet strong against the prideful. I pray that those leaders in the church today who have not been in chains to porn will see their own sin in light of a Holy God and remember some of the most important truths of the scriptures, namely, that "Christ died for the ungodly," which is you and I.

"For when we were still without strength, in due time Christ died for the ungodly" (Romans 5:6, NKJV).

AMPUTATION

I love Jesus! He's so radical. I mean just look at some of the things he said, like: "If your eye causes you to sin, pluck it out."

For all of us into porn, this is needed and required. To not do this would bring about no change and worldly regret, leading to death. In 2 Corinthians 7, when Paul describes the repentance of a man in the church, he says, "What indignation!" But what does that mean? *Indignation* is a word that means a righteous wrath. When a child is killed by a mass murderer, we have an indignation inside of us screaming, "Justice!"

In the passage mentioned, this indignation was a visible sign of a person's change of mind toward the things of God. He had indignation. What was his indignation? I believe it was toward the sexual bondage he was in, if indeed this is the same gentlemen that was mentioned in the first letter to the Corinthian church in chapter 5; he was having sex with his father's wife! Sounds pretty pornographic to me. The most famous porn video, or close to it, was the Taboo flicks that came out in the seventies, where mom and son were involved sexually. Once again, the Bible is way ahead of the culture today.

Paul says elsewhere that we are to hate even the garment defiled by the flesh. This means that we are to have hatred, a passionate, gut-reaching desire to get rid of anything that will keep us in bondage. The word that describes that action is *indignation*.

We are to seek God to receive an indignation for porn that results in such a radical action that people around us see it as being a bit too much or foolish. For some, this might look like getting rid of the cable box, which has been used to access porn videos at $15.00 a pop. Or it might be putting a filter on your computer. And to your embarrassment, you have to explain why you have a filter on that is preventing your friends or family from visiting YouTube or Photobucket or any other networking, file sharing sites.

It could be even more radical as to throw out your computer or your TV or even rip up your credit cards or give your cards to your spouse so you are unable to use them. I remember when I was taking a purity course in 2007, the founder of the ministry was sharing his testimony about amputation. As a pilot, he was in hotel after hotel where adult videos would constantly be a temptation. Finally, by grace, he amputated by unhooking the TV and setting it outside in the hall. Explaining why he had to do that would have been quite tough, but because Christ was of infinite value to him, it was done. Radical amputation is not just removing, but with the same action, godly amputation is replacing what is being amputated. Jesus says, "He who loses anything for my sake gains me. He who hates his mother and father gains the Kingdom. Blessed are the blind, for they shall see." This is such a common theme in the teaching of Jesus. Amputation means gaining Christ. It's with joy that we give up everything because we gain all.

Many throughout the Bible have amputated something in just this way. Joseph fled from the Potipher's wife, Moses left the riches (and women) of Egypt, and Daniel, while in Babylon, remained pure, giving up all that the government of Babylon had to offer. Yet they sought a kingdom that is not of this world, a better place.

For me this meant leaving my future wife to seek something better!

When I was 19, I was deeply involved in a relationship with a wonderful girl whom I had known since I was eight. She happened to live four houses from mine. Though we were friends growing up, it wasn't until I was in college that we began dating. As a believer in the Lord, I had a desire to serve Him, yet all too many times I would fall into sexual sin with my girlfriend. This would happen over and over and the guilt just mounted and mounted. On top of other compromises in my walk at the time were the pressures of being a full-time college student. I could not keep this life up, and I knew it. I recall getting on my knees once again in the middle of the night, all alone, and crying out to the Lord. It was a bit like Psalm 50:15, "Call upon Me in the day of trouble; I will deliver you, and you shall glorify Me" (NKJV). The next day I received a call from my second father from Kauai, Hawaii, asking if I would like to move out there! I said, yes, knowing that this was a open door to cut off the areas of sin that I had allowed to creep into life. The next step was explaining this to my girlfriend. All I could say was that I needed to go and get with the Lord. I let her know that she could do whatever she wanted, that she had no commitment to me in any way. I had to make the cut.

This was radical. Here I was in love, and she was too, yet I let her become an idol, and God will not be rivaled by any. How many are afraid to cut off for fear of losing it all? A.W. Tozer, in the Pursuit of God, said that "we are often hindered from giving up our treasures to the Lord out of fear for their safety; this is especially true when those treasures are loved relatives and friends (or in my case my beautiful girlfriend). But we need have no such fears. Our Lord came not to destroy but to save. Everything is safe which we commit to Him, and nothing is really safe which is not so committed."

Amputation is gaining more of God.

> There is nothing I desire besides you.
> Psalm 73:25 (NKJV)

> With joy he sold all to gain the treasure.
> Matthew 13:55 (paraphrase)

> They are abundantly satisfied with the fullness of your house, and you give them drink from the river of your pleasures.
> Psalm 36:8 (NKJV)

And this is where I leave off. Being free of porn happens when we enjoy God, who is of greater value, more pleasurable, and satisfying.

God is more pleasurable and satisfying than porn.

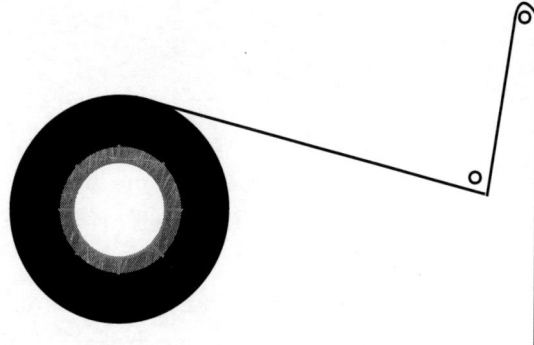

CONCLUSION

My hope in writing this book is for all to learn a bit about the porn industry and its influence on a bona fide life: mine. Also it is, I believe, an addition to the books that I have quoted on the porn industry.¹ This addition to the topic of Porn is not only from a pastor who ministers to people in bondage to porn, but a pastor who is open to say that he has been in bondage to it as well. So my perspective is not just academic, but my heart weighs with all that

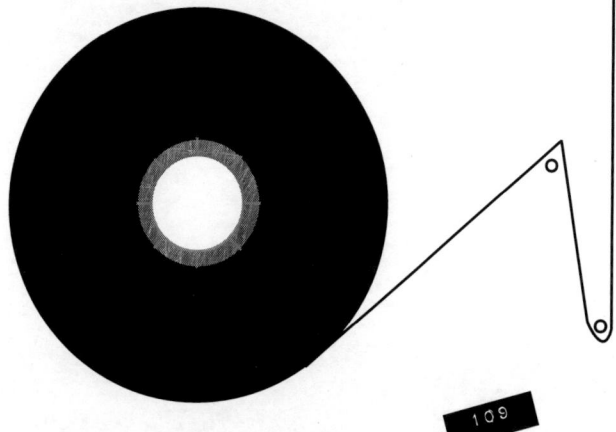

I've said. I haven't just done metal gymnastics in writing about porn but have been moved emotionally and relationally by its influence in my life.

My heart goes out to all my friends I grew up with. I think of them often.

Above all, I would hope those in my world of the American Christian church would give this a read and prayerfully consider its contents in relation to what we believe is the Word of God. For my generation is the next group of pastors, elders, deacons, and teachers in the church. And like it or not, this has been our lives. We have grown up around the Red Hot Chili Peppers and porn. It's a different generation, if, by the grace of God, we can see Jesus as such a pleasure and of great reward, and to be greatly valued.

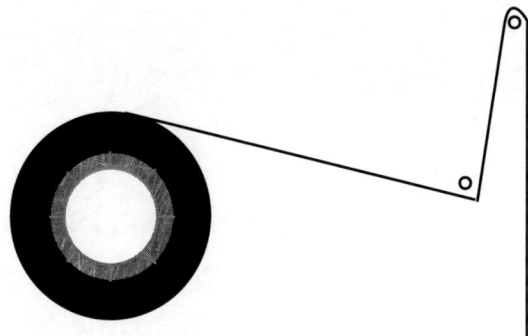

ENDNOTES

1. http://www.foxbusiness.com/story/markets/economy/adult-entertainment-industry-wants-bailout/
2. http://porninthevalley.com/2008/11/03/porn-stars-are-the-new-crossover-artists.aspx
3. http://www.timesonline.co.uk/tol/news/article567762.ece

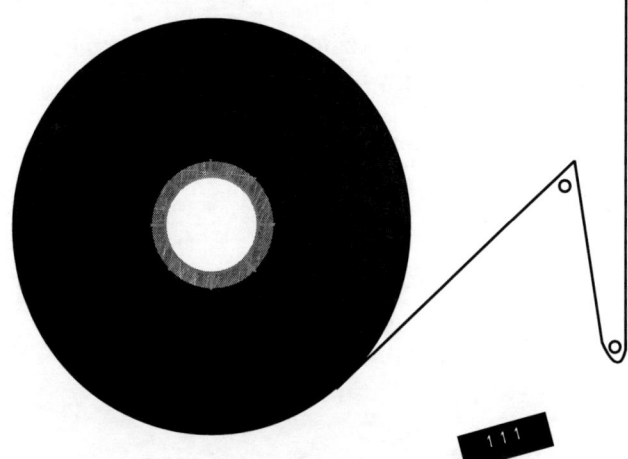

4. http://www.christianpost.com/article/20081103/study-teen-pregnancies-tied-to-tastes-for-sex-laced-tv/index.html

5. http://www.ciol.com/News/News-Reports/Toon-porn-star-Savita-bhabhi-under-fire/29508106534/0/

6. http://news.bbc.co.uk/go/pr/fr/-/2/hi/technology/3041022.stm

7. http://www.thingsasian.com/stories-photos/3141

8. http://www.int.iol.co.za/index.php?click_id=13&set_id=1&art_id=vn20080816083221147C411936

9. The Porning of America pg. 201

10. http://www.int.iol.co.za/index.php?sf=3&click_id=3&art_id=qw990444181879B265&set_id=1

11. http://www.mnweekly.ru/columnists/20080619/55333926.html

12. http://www.somethingjewish.co.uk/articles/2605_sexy_israeli_festiva.htm

13. http://www.zionism-israel.com/israel_news/2007/07/porn-substitutes-for-sex-in-palestinian.html

14. http://www.zionism-israel.com/israel_news/2007/07/porn-substitutes-for-sex-in-palestinian.html

15. http://internet-filter-review.toptenreviews.com/internet-pornography-statistics.html

16. http://www.ocf.berkeley.edu/~lilylin/TomorrowLegislation.htm

17. http://www.eros.org.au/index.php?option=com_content&task=view&id=2&Itemid=2
18. http://app1.chinadaily.com.cn/star/2001/0809/fe20-1.html
19. http://www.alleyinsider.com/2008/7/where-the-government-tax-rebate-checks-really-went-porn
20. http://en.wikipedia.org/wiki/Generation_X
21. http://www.familysafemedia.com/pornography_statistics.html
22. http://education.yahoo.com/reference/dictionary/entry/addiction
23. http://www.safefamilies.org/sfStats.php
24. http://www.safefamilies.org/sfStats.php
25. Ceil, Memoirs of the Rev. John Newton, p. 105
26. http://deseretnews.com/article/1,5143,600158179,00.html?pg=1
27. http://www.desiringgod.org/ResourceLibrary/Sermons/ByDate/2001/68_Set_Free_by_the_Spirit_of_Life_in_Christ_Jesus/